TH SMALL BUSINESS OWNER'S BIBLE

3 IN 1

The Ultimate Guide on How to Start, Run, and Grow
your LLC or S-Corp | Including Everything You
Need to Know About Quickbooks

THOMAS NEWTON

Thank You
for your purchase!

SCAN THIS QR CODE BELOW to get your

4 FREE BONUS to boost your productivity **in only 7 days!**

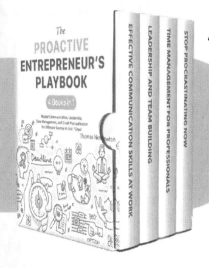

SCAN ME

» BOOK 1: HOW TO SET UP YOUR PERFECT OFFICE AT HOME

» BOOK 2: TIME MANAGEMENT FOR PROFESSIONALS

» BOOK 3: STOP PROCRASTINATING NOW!

» BOOK 4: EFFECTIVE COMMUNICATION SKILLS AT WORK

Good work and best of luck
with your business!

Thomas

TABLE OF CONTENTS

LLC BEGINNER'S GUIDE 2024

The Most Updated Guide on How to Start, Grow, and Run your Single-Member Limited Liability Company.

THOMAS NEWTON

INTRODUCTION

Welcome to the journey of being a part of an LLC. An LLC is a Limited Liability Company. If you pay attention to small businesses, you've probably noticed a lot of company names with LLCs written at the end. An LLC is a business structure that allows individuals to benefit from tax laws while also providing a level of security typically reserved for larger corporations.

The main element that an LLC shares with a corporation are its limited liability components.

It is critical to remember that the formation of an LLC does not imply that the newly formed entity is a corporation; rather, it provides the business structure with some of the benefits that a corporation enjoys.

An LLC is more accurately identified as a voluntary association. A voluntary association sounds self-explanatory but has a deeper meaning, like most business terms. A voluntary association is the formation of a group to achieve specific goals to protect the business members. In the case of an LLC, the goals may be directed toward having a distinct business rather than just a hobby income stream.

Because an LLC is described as a type of association, it has some flexibility. This adaptability is best demonstrated when deciding how to run your business daily. This structure allows each business member to participate in decision-making, or at the very least allows the members to select a member or group to manage the business's operations. It is even possible for someone not part of the managing or executive command structure to run the business.

Unlike other forms of formal business models, individuals involved in an LLC are not required to organize formal meetings or prepare written documentation of the meetings so that they can be reviewed in an audit later.

However, your LLC should hold annual meetings of the board of corporate directors and shareholders.

The decisions made at these meetings should be documented in writing. This is a simple way for those involved in the LLC to protect its members and those with a financial interest in the LLC from personal liability for the professional actions of the business while conducting official business.

| CHAPTER 1 |

THE BENEFITS OF LLC FOR SMALL BUSINESS OWNERS

I t is no longer a secret that most SMEs prefer an LLC as their business entity. The benefits of an LLC are straightforward, given that multiple factors are critical in forming a limited liability company: the intermediate cost and effort required to continue forming an LLC. But what is the benefit of an LLC for a small business owner?

An LLC can be easily formed privately with minimum expenses by simply locating and adding your company information with template posts. It takes approximately 15 minutes.

Selecting a limited liability company (LLC) as a business structure offers several advantages to all sorts of businesses. Business owners that incorporate as an LLC do so via their state, so the procedures and expenses differ slightly, but the benefits are consistent: personal liability protection, flexibility in operational and taxing structure, and broad eligibility.

BENEFITS OF LLC

Suitable for individuals

The benefits of an LLC are not limited to multi-member businesses. Individuals might also profit from forming a single-member LLC. You receive personal asset protection and more control over how you choose to be taxed. For certain firms, deciding to be taxed as an S corp may result in tax savings; however, state restrictions regarding S corp status differ, and so do your local study.

Personal liability protection

Among the most significant advantages of creating an LLC is that it isolates your personal assets from those of the business. This protects your house, vehicle, and money if your company is sued or fails on a loan.

A personal guarantee for company finance is an exception. That does allow creditors to make you personally liable for debt repayment. Furthermore, if there is proof of fraud or negligence causing injury to people concerned, you might be held personally liable in a lawsuit.

Cheaper & surprisingly simple to form

Starting a business as an LLC is relatively simple and affordable compared to corporations. The particular procedure is controlled by your state, although the paperwork and expense are usually modest. In addition to completing a brief formation document, you'll need to file articles of organization and an operating agreement explaining the new company's ownership structure. Templates for them may be accessible online, so you don't have to start from scratch.

Because of the lower operational complexity, incorporating an LLC is typically more enticing to small firms than founding a corporation. LLCs are not obligated to have an annual shareholders' meeting or file an annual report.

Pliable Taxation

Selecting an LLC as your entity type provides you with several possibilities for paying taxes. Only if an LLC elects to be taxed as C corporation profits are passed through to the owners as personal income rather than corporate taxes, this is known as pass-through taxes, and it saves money by avoiding double taxation (at the corporate level and the personal level).

But, depending on your tax categorization, you may be required to pay self-employment taxes.

The QBI (qualified business income) deduction, a recent tax law modification, also enables many LLCs to qualify for a Federal Tax Deduction on pass-through revenue. Business owners with pass-through income can deduct up to 20% of their net income on their federal tax returns until 2025.

Flexibility in ownership and management

Members of an LLC company structure can decide how earnings are distributed. In contrast, a general partnership compels all partners to divide corporate earnings equally. Instead, LLCs allow earnings to be divided according to the operating agreement's provisions. If one member puts in more money upfront or more sweat equity (performing the hard work of bringing the firm to maturity), the agreement may offer them a bigger share of the earnings.

Furthermore, the number of owners in an LLC is not restricted. There is also no necessity for a governing body, such as a board of directors or a group of executives, as a corporation would.

USING A DEMAND LETTER TO BENEFIT YOUR LLC

Are you familiar with a letter of request and how your company can benefit from it? When you form an LLC, you ensure that every customer pays every bill on time. When you form an LLC, any customers will simply refuse to pay. However, before going to court, try writing a letter outlining your request. This will help you get the desired results while saving money and time. Demand letters assist in resolving 30% of all future conflicts between LLCs and other companies. The beauty of a letter of request is that it is inexpensive and simple to write; it is a simple, concise letter requesting payment. If the consumer does not pay or no agreement is reached, you will have additional paperwork to present to a court.

People do not expect a small company owner to tackle the debt with the same rigor as a big company. Thus, they will sadly neglect your polite attempts to obtain payments. A letter from your LLC states why you owe, what you owe, and the legal alternative if you don't pay. This shows that you are serious and willing to appear before the court. Sometimes, the prospect of appearing before the judge and facing your debt publicly is enough to make people pay; however, you want to avoid court as much as possible.

The best way to represent your LLC is through a well-written letter. To make the request letter successful, you want to include a few main items:

- A debt history. While the client should know why it owes it and the efforts you have made to recover it, it does provide a comprehensive history for the judge if you must go to court.
- Enter the unique results you are looking for. E.g., '$250.00 must be completely paid on or before July 1.'
- Professional look and sound. Your letter of request represents your LLC. Type a letter on the letterhead of the company. Avoid misrepresentation and keep the content company linked. Retain a copy of your documents.
- Conclude your letter by stating that you intend to take legal action if your request is not fulfilled. E.g., "If the full amount is not paid before July 1, $250 will be added to the amount immediately."

In an ideal world, you provide good products, and, in return, the customer pays promptly. If that does not apply to your situation, consider submitting a request letter and utilizing your valuable time to run your LLC.

AN EXPLANATION OF LLCS & DISADVANTAGES

Limited Liability Companies or LLCs are among the most common company forms for entrepreneurs who start new projects. If you have ever looked at the names of companies selling products and services, some of them may have corporate names that end in "LLC." An LLC is a company type. If you've ever considered starting your own business, this is one of your options. However, before registering your business in this manner, you should learn more about LLCs to determine whether they are the right type of company for you.

The founders of the LLC, also known as "members," are not directly responsible for the company's debts and costs. You may ask, "But don't other business types, like corporations, have this form of protection?" Yes, other business types may provide limited liability to you, but the LLC has other advantages.

To begin with, it's very easy to create. Most states have forms that you can only download if you send them in. Your pay fees are usually negligible in most countries (unless you want to process them quickly). In the long run, the records and documents required by LLCs are usually simpler.

With LLC, you can vote for taxes. You could choose to be taxed as a partnership, S Company, or C Company. This flexibility is attractive for many business owners, especially those who want to profit from cheaper taxes.

You don't have to worry about double taxation when it comes to taxes unless you choose to be taxed as a C Corporation or form your LLC in the District of Columbia. You are only charged with the same salary once. This benefit makes LLC an enticing option for people who run a freelance or consulting enterprise.

Even with its numerous benefits, an LLC still has a few disadvantages. One big downside is that you cannot sell the company's stocks or shares. This makes expanding difficult, especially for companies that expect to be published one day. Furthermore, if one owner wishes to leave the company, the LLC and the remaining owners must be dissolved. If they want to continue operating together, the LLC must be reformed again.

The LLC is also a new organization. As a result, it lacks the reputation of trust associated with a company or other type of enterprise. This makes finding capital more difficult if you are looking for external investors. This also means that national laws on LLCs vary because there is no agreement on how the government should handle them fiscally and administratively.

As you can see, LLCs have perks and drawbacks like any other company structure. The business owner decides if the benefits of creating an LLC are worth the disadvantages you face.

| CHAPTER 2 |

HOW TO START AN LLC

A Limited Liability Company, as opposed to a sole proprietorship or corporation, provides additional legal protection. They usually stand out from their owners.

Filing as an LLC requires additional steps and documentation, which vary by state. You may be charged a fee to send these documents. Although forming an LLC takes more time and money, it provides greater security, which you may want in the event of an accident.

An organization, like an LLC, needs paperwork detailing people's positions within the business. Corporations comprise stockholders who own the company, directors who control it, and officers who manage its day-to-day operations.

Your company would typically need to apply bylaws and articles of incorporation to register as a corporation, but the exact requirements vary by state. Corporations are taxed differently than other types of businesses.

Corporations are the most complex entity in terms of legal work, but they also have the most security. A corporation may be the best option if you have multiple owners or expect significant growth.

STEPS IN FORMING LLC

One of the most significant stages in starting a business is forming a limited liability company (LLC). An LLC can provide your company with liability protection in addition to other benefits. In contrast, the specific procedures for forming an LLC vary substantially by state. Following are some basic guidelines about what to expect throughout the procedure.

Select a State

LLCs can be incorporated in any 50 states, irrespective of where you live or want to do business. Among the fifty states, Delaware, Nevada, and Wyoming laws are among the most business-friendly. Income earned outside of Delaware is not subject to taxation in that state. Business income is not taxed in Nevada or Wyoming. A first-time business owner will frequently select one of these three states when incorporating an LLC.

However, evading the taxman is not so simple. If you incorporate in any of these states, there is a good probability that you will wind up paying more overall.

If business companies could evade business income taxes simply by incorporating Nevada or Wyoming, everyone would do so.

We strongly advise creating your LLC in your native state.

There are three main reasons why you should avoid incorporating your new LLC outside of your native state:

- You'll still have to pay your home state taxes.
- You will have to pay twice for registered agents, annual filings, franchise taxes, and other expenses.
- It's simply inconvenient.

Naming your LLC

As you evaluate business names, marketing may be at the forefront of your mind. While picking the proper name for branding considerations is critical, your business name must also comply with state legislation. Find a name that makes sense for your company.

In any case, you may always register a DBA, sometimes called a Fictitious Business Name (FBA). DBAs enable you to use any name as your trade name.

Your LLC name remains the same as a DBA, but your brand name might differ.

Prerequisites for Naming

State regulations differ significantly. However, the respective standards are universal:

- It must be a distinct name.
- The phrase "LLC," "Limited Liability Company," or "Ltd." must be included.
- It cannot include terms or phrases that may be mistaken with government agencies, such as the Police Department, IRS, Department of State, etc.
- It cannot contain protected terms like "college," "hospital," or "bank" unless there is a compelling cause to do so.

Select a Registered Agent

You need to have a registered agent, either an individual or a business, to act as the official contact for your limited liability company.

Official communication and service of process (legal papers connected to litigation) will always be sent to the postal address of your registered agent by government entities and attorneys.

Individuals over 18 can be registered agents if they have a physical address in the state where your LLC was created. Companies can also be registered agents.

You can legally appoint yourself as your LLC's registered agent.

We highly advise you not to appoint yourself.

The registered agent information is open to the public and may be seen online. If you value your privacy, never appoint yourself.

It is best to choose a third party as your registered agent. That third party is typically a legal firm or a registered agent service.

Typically, registered agent businesses charge around $120 per year to act as your registered agent. Attorneys frequently charge extra, sometimes up to $500 per year.

File Articles of Organization

You will be required to submit papers to the state agency that handles company filings in your state to create your LLC as a legal organization. When you file articles of formation with your Secretary of State, your limited liability corporation is legally constituted. In certain states, these articles are also called a certificate of formation or a certificate of organization.

Documents required for formation must include:

- The LLC's business address
- The LLC's registered agent's name and address
- The founding member's name & address details
- Whether your LLC is administered by members or by non-members
- Effective date
- Validity of your LLC, if you wish it to expire at a specific date
- Business Purpose Statement

The articles can be filed by mail or online. The actual filing fee will differ from state to state. When submitting this document, you must supply accurate information.

Online formation providers manage the full LLC creation or incorporation procedure from beginning to end. It's the easiest and quickest approach to establishing a limited liability company. Since they handle everything digitally, they may save money by filing everything themselves rather than hiring an attorney or certified public accountant.

Draft an Operating Agreement

If you are creating your own limited liability company (LLC), the operating agreement is the single most crucial document. It establishes the ground principles for how your organization operates internally and with the public. As a result, ensuring that your business structure works for you is critical.

Although most states do not require LLCs to have operating agreements, having one is vital to get your firm off to a good start and offer it the best chance of success.

A limited liability company's objective is to protect your personal assets. Personal assets such as automobiles, residences, and money are not in danger if your company is sued or goes bankrupt.

Furthermore, without personal liability protection, your company organization is more akin to a sole proprietorship, which means creditors can seize your personal assets. The end effect might be disastrous for both your business and your life.

The LLC operating agreement explicitly states your, the other LLC members, and the company's connection. It guarantees that the LLC company structure fully protects you and the other members and that the firm functions smoothly.

Operating agreements provide these safeguards in a variety of ways:

- They define the rights and responsibilities of LLC members. The operating agreement for a limited liability company should state whether or not a single member of the LLC is responsible for day-to-day operations and record keeping.
- What is a non-member manager permitted to accomplish? Managers are held to higher standards of accountability by the company and its members. The operating agreement is where these details can be laid down.
- What the LLC is lawfully entitled to. The operating agreement should also specify how the company may perform its operations daily.

- How new employees can join the organization. They also set guidelines for how an LLC member can depart.
- When and how revenues are distributed to members. They can also design various forms of membership and payment programs.
- Whether members or management in charge, they also guide how to hire and terminate managers.
- How and under what conditions should the LLC be terminated? You may not wish to dissolve your company right now, but you may in the future. It's wise to think about it and plan ahead of time before it becomes a problem.
- How to Modify the Rules In the future, you may need to revise your LLC operating agreement. The operating agreement should specify how adjustments will be made.

When you look at the laws of most states, you'll see that they frequently have their own "default" regulations for how these things work in an LLC. In most circumstances, operating agreements allow you to tailor the regulations to your own scenario.

If you do not have an LLC operating agreement and something unexpected occurs, the future of your LLC may be determined by what state legislation is in effect at the time. With your contract in place, you get control of your firm and its destiny.

Putting together an operating agreement may be daunting. The easiest way to go about it is to consult a lawyer or business formation agency about your company's requirements.

Obtain an EIN

An Employer Identification Number (EIN) is your LLC's nine-digit tax identification number. Consider it your LLC's social security number. The IRS uses these numbers to maintain track of business organizations for tax purposes.

The government requires EINs for any LLCs that produce money or wish to hire staff. Most financial institutions require an EIN when opening a business bank account.

You must submit an EIN application to the IRS. Applications can be submitted using the SS-4 form via mail or online. Once completing the online form, you will get EIN instantly.

An EIN is not required for single-member LLCs. You can substitute your social security number. However, we strongly advise having an EIN to protect your identity and separate your personal and corporate funds.

LLC AS AN INDIVIDUAL

A person with CLL is someone who wishes to form an LLC. It is a hybrid business structure that shares characteristics with both a corporation and a sole proprietorship. Its owners, like those of a corporation, have personal protection. The company's debts do not affect its assets. Profits and losses are declared in the income tax declaration for the sole owner in the same way for single ownership.

A sole proprietorship is a business owned and operated by a single individual. The default is unique if it does not act as a Limited Liability Company or Corporation and does not have a single owner. As previously stated, all gains, losses, expenses, and business deductions are reported on the owner's tax return because the company does not pay corporate tax.

THE RULES OF A SINGLE MEMBER LLC

The Limited Liability Corporation may be a perplexing business structure as an appealing association. A few significant differences distinguish the LLC from the standard (or limited liability) format.

Individual LLC members are distinguished from ordinary LLCs because the former has only one member, owner, or manager. The technological gap closes here, but there are a few other possibilities.

Note: Not all states will allow you to join a single LLC member. You will be asked to form a sole proprietorship that you form instead. This is unfortunate because it limits limited liability rights. It is, however, a factor. The good news is that you do not have to live in a state to organize your company (you simply want to do business there), so your geographical location is not an impediment. For example, you could live in Nevada and form an LLC in Delaware, similar to how the company does.

A Risky Endeavor

Unfortunately, because LLCs (i.e., partnerships) exist, some of the benefits of LLCs are not usually realized by their members. Many legal professionals would allow you to establish a relationship with your organization even if you only give a close family member or friend 2% of your business. This is due to several complex rules and laws.

Charge Order Protection

The government forbids your creditors from seizing corporate assets to protect them. Rather, you can only demand your share of the Company's income. You create this complex by constructing an SMLLC. As a result, you can avoid this by filling out IRS Form 8832 and electing to have your company taxed as a corporation.

Death and Operating Agreements

As a sole member of an LLC, the organization is subject to several restrictions (partly because this type of business has emerged as an alternative to a partnership). A significant but often overlooked advantage of businesses is that their lives are unrelated to the lives or well-being of a single person. When an owner (stockholder) passes away, the company simply redistributes its ownership and continues to operate.

Multi-partner LLCs operate in the same way that regular LLCs do, but single LLCs do not. In this case, the operating contract must specify who will take over ownership in the event of the owner's death. The individuals will usually support this.

Tax Time

Single LLCs also have their own set of tax rules. The IRS regards the arrangement as an unrecognized entity and taxes LLCs with one owner in the same way it charges sole property.

As always, take notes and keep your personal and business finances separate. This is true for all organizations, but it is especially important when shaping and operating an LLC as a single member of complicated situations.

Although many people do not recommend operating as a single LLC member, other types of activity are possible and potentially better. Always keep track of the complicated state of affairs as you work and brace yourself (or the will) for a headache.

START-UP CHOICE: CORPORATION INC OR LLC?

LLC Vs. Partnership

This association article refers to two business entities: a Limited Liability Company and a partnership. While they are similar legal forms, they differ in personal responsibility, management controls, formal processes, and other features.

Association Against LLC: Differences and Similarities

A Limited Liability Company (LLC) is a popular business entity that shares characteristics with other legal structures known as partnerships. They are similar in terms of how they were formed and the "pass-through" method of taxation, but they differ in terms of characteristics such as participant responsibility.

What is an Association?

An Association is a kind of business with many partners who are necessarily co-owners. To form a company:

- You must have 2 or more parties agree to have the company operate for profit.
- Partners share management activities and share gains and financial losses of the company.
- The amount of income depends on the individual owner's initial investment.

Several partnerships exist, depending on the industry and the owners' desires.

Forming an LLC entails registering the business in the state where it is located as a partnership. Most Limited Liability Companies operate based on an operating agreement, which specifies the percentage of questions from members and answers to "what if?" questions. An LLC is a taxation by-pass style of a partnership or sole proprietorship that lacks the benefit of personal responsibility and is as limited as a society.

PERSONAL, LIMITED LIABILITY

Personal, Limited Liability means its owners divide their assets and judgments against the company. The owners' personal property, such as a car or home, cannot be touched by creditors if the company receives a lawsuit or a debt that jeopardizes the organization. Owners' illegal, unethical, or reckless behavior results in the cancellation of the limited liability protection.

Many people consider the LLC format an ideal combination of a partnership and a corporation, given its distinguishing characteristics. It is a hybrid corporate-individual business structure.

CHAPTER 3

IS AN LLC RIGHT FOR ME?

The decision to form an LLC or take your business in another direction could be the key to your company's success. Legalzoom.com stated, "When an owner establishes the LLC, startup costs are low, and there is less paperwork than there is when starting a corporation. If an LLC is properly operated, and its assets and agreements are in the business's name, the members will not be personally liable for the actions and debts of the business."

This is a compelling reason a company should consider incorporating it as an LLC. One of the most important reasons to form an LLC is to protect yourself and your family from some financial risks associated with running a business.

One of the advantages of forming an LLC as the owner or founder of the company is that the initial startup costs are low. Another advantage of forming an LLC is that significantly less paperwork is required than forming a corporation. It is critical to ensure that your LLC is properly managed.

This ensures that your business and its assets and agreements are in the business's name. The proper operation and filing of the essential paperwork will allow your members to not be personally liable for the actions and debts of the business. These are some of the benefits of forming an LLC.

While there aren't many disadvantages to running your business as an LLC, it's important to understand that some obligations may not be the best fit for your company or your expectations of what an LLC can do for you. Some of the components of an LLC that must be fully considered include the fact that there will be ongoing expenses to maintain the LLC.

These costs, however, will apply to other types of business structures, such as corporations and partnerships. Even if taxes on the LLC's income are often passed through to the individual members, the LLC must still file tax returns.

One advantage that may be important to your business is that the owners of an LLC are not required to reside in the United States. When forming an LLC, there is no legal residency requirement. If you are not a citizen or permanent resident of the United States, this could be another plus in your favor when deciding whether an LLC is right for your business.

The ability to remain an LLC, relocate outside of the United States, or have members of your LLC located in or from various parts of the world may be the best fit for your company, especially if your business caters to non-U.S. citizen-clients.

The credibility that comes with becoming an LLC is one of the less tangible factors that must be considered when deciding whether you want or need to form your business into a legally recognized business. When a company applies for or becomes an official business entity, it can positively impact how others perceive your company.

Taking the time and spending money to form an LLC demonstrates that your business is a serious entity, not a side project. Vendors, suppliers, and other professional services contractors will be less wary of doing business with a company that appears to take its responsibilities seriously. The organization's owners and members have taken responsible precautions to protect themselves.

Your potential and current customers, like your vendors, may be concerned about the legitimacy of your company. Customers are more likely to trust your company if they believe you and your company are fully invested in your product or service. Customers are sold on your confidence by displaying that your company is an LLC.

Another disadvantage of forming an LLC is that ownership in an LLC is often more difficult to transfer than in other business structures, such as a corporation. This gives all members of the LLC, regardless of their ownership stake in the company, a similar amount of power when it comes to adding new members to the LLC.

The most significant disadvantage of forming an LLC is reducing the growth potential. Every year, many business owners strive to expand their operations and achieve greater levels of success. An LLC limits this growth for some business models because it does not allow for the distribution of shares in the LLC to attract potential investors.

While this is a significant disadvantage for some business owners considering incorporating their company as an LLC, it is not always a deal-breaker. It could be an option if your company is new and in its early stages. Creating a new legal structure for your company is always possible, but this is a time-consuming and costly process.

The LLC structure is a newer business model in the United States. This novelty generates an interesting debate as to whether it is positive or negative. This is because the court system has yet to rule on some issues that may arise with your LLC. This is not a major concern for your company at this time, as the benefits of an LLC outweigh the potential risk of entering an area of the legal system where some of the gray areas of operating an LLC have not yet been fully resolved.

It is best to take your time in the early stages of determining which path is right for your company. Making a list of your company's goals can help you decide what legal structure will work best for you in the short and long term.

Consulting with a corporate lawyer about your plans is never a bad idea. However, this is not always necessary. Joining a local small business owners' group is another excellent source of information and support. There, you will be able to discuss the benefits and drawbacks of your company, as well as what types of corporate structures will work best for you.

Odds are your business will benefit from becoming an LLC, but make sure that you and your partners have taken the appropriate due diligence to ensure that you are doing what is best for your business, yourself, and your partners.

WHAT'S THE DIFFERENCE BETWEEN A BUSINESS'S LEGAL STRUCTURE AND TAX STRUCTURE?

- The tax structure is handled by the IRS on a federal basis, while your state handles the company structure.
- The IRS does not accept LLCs, even though you register as one with the department. You may be classified as a sole proprietor, partnership, S-corporation, or C-corporation for tax purposes.
- Under the LLC, you will get all the defense advantages, but the tax process differs.
- You can save money on FICA (Federal Insurance Contributions Act) payments, also known as payroll taxes, and escape double taxation by forming an S-corporation.

The company owner usually shapes the company with dire tax implications without consulting an experienced company or a tax consultant. Even the NYS State Division of Companies Website mentions this fact: "Therefore, it is advisable to review, with a close look at the tax consequences, the business situation when deciding which organization to form."

In fact, many LLCs have been created for the wrong reasons, with catastrophic consequences for companies and their owners who will bear the burden of that decision for years to come and probably decades to come.

A Limited Liability Company is the combination of a company and a partnership. They closely mimic and are taxed like partnerships but are limited liability benefits like companies.

They are established by registering a unique name through the secretary of state in the state where the company is located. Each state has its particular rules and fee schedules for forming one. The cost of establishing an LLC in NYS is considerably more due to the need to publish a notice of intent.

An LLC is formed by paying a fee and filing articles of the organization with the appropriate state office. It can be established in several states by filing a simple one-page document that sets out the LLC's Articles of Organization. The new LLC must choose a name, a place for its headquarters, and the names of all of its founding members. Some states will also require LLCs to announce the business's expected duration, file an operating agreement, and provide other legally required details. Annual fees and filing requirements are also common.

Some corporations, such as banks and insurance companies, cannot be LLC, just as they cannot be an S company. Unlike an S corporation, however, an LLC may have members that are corporations, associations, or even foreign organizations (there are some special rules for foreign-owned LLCs). In addition, unlike an S company, the number of owners/members of the business is unrestricted. Most states recognize them as separate entity forms for tax purposes, but the federal government does not recognize them as such. As a result, it may specify how it wants to be handled by the IRS for tax purposes. The IRS will treat an LLC with one member (or a single-member LLC) as a sole proprietorship for tax purposes unless otherwise stated, and the IRS will "disregard" it as an entity form. An LLC disregarded object is what this is called. This ignored status has no bearing on liability protection; it simply instructs the IRS and the taxpayer that taxes should be charged as though they did not exist. By default, the IRS can consider an LLC with more than one member (or a multi-member LLC) as a partnership. An IRS Form 8832 should be filed if it wishes to be treated as a C company. If there is some doubt on how the IRS will handle it for tax purposes, Form 8832 allows the LLC to designate how the company should be taxed directly. A company, association, sole proprietor, disregarded entity, domestic entity, or international entity are the choices available on that form. However, the LLC must meet the prerequisite conditions for becoming an S corporation, which includes filing Form 8832 and opting to be treated as a corporation.

Converting business forms necessitates some advanced legal and tax research, which you can do with the assistance of an attorney and accountant.

The person from whom you want to be treated as within your LLC determines the IRS taxation rules you must obey on a federal level. If you don't make a selection and have a single-member LLC, you'll be subject to the sole proprietor/self-employed taxation laws, and if you have a multiple-member LLC, you'll be subject to the general partnership taxation rules.

To ensure that it receives the proper tax treatment, you must file IRS Form 8832, which specifies the tax treatment for your LLC. Suppose you want to be categorized as an S corporation. In that case, you must first choose to be "listed as an organization taxable as a corporation" on IRS Form 8832 and then apply IRS Form 2553 to specify further that you want to be treated as an S corporation. These are time-sensitive documents, so send them as soon as possible to ensure IRS acceptance of your chosen selection.

CHAPTER 4

LLC: INCORPORATING SUCCESS IN YOUR BUSINESS

B y forming an LLC, industries ranging from real estate to construction will reap numerous benefits and provide the company and its customers with more opportunities.

When establishing a company, an LLC is a company structure that allows your company to have legal liability similar to that of a corporation while avoiding annual reports, share distributions, regulations, and other requirements.

Forming an LLC is especially advantageous for new businesses. It combines a relationship's control and tax advantages with the least amount of transparency. Members of an LLC are frequently protected from corporate liability or lawsuits. An LLC is more adaptable than a corporation because its members can include foreign individuals, trusts, associations, businesses, and non-residents. Furthermore, maintenance is simple; an LLC has fewer formalities and is easier to operate than a corporation.

VARIATIONS IN THE LLC RELATIVE TO THE BUSINESS

- Companies are owned by ownership shares or inventories that are distributed to shareholders. Like partnerships, an LLC belongs to its members or managers.
- In comparison to LLC, businesses need annual meetings and written minutes. LLC requires less paperwork because these standards do not apply.
- A company must pay income taxes on its earnings at the corporate tax rate. An LLC is a "pass-through" tax agency, on the other hand. The gains or losses generated by the corporation shall appear on the owners' income tax returns. Therefore, the double taxation of corporate and personal income tax payable is avoided.

WHAT TO EXPECT AFTER FILING AN LLC

Once you have opted to apply for an LLC, the paperwork will be clarified in two articles with a CD. They will come along with the corporate or LLC pack.

The Organizational Articles formalize your life by following the laws of the state. After you've filed this, you'll have a legal company up and running.

This document specifies the company's name, intent, incorporators, quantities, stock types that may be issued, and any other unique characteristics. On the other hand, the operating agreement includes the LLC's written code of conduct. Meetings, board and officer appointments, notices, forms and duties, and a standard procedure are required.

There will also be a registered agent who can accept official documents on your behalf. Examples of documents received are tax advisories, annual reports, and documents relating to the legal process, such as appeals.

The final steps include submitting an amendment article to reflect the shift of your business from a company to an LLC. You must also submit an original or annual report. Experts in business filing may assist in the processing of required business changes.

CHOICE OF BUSINESS ENTITY

The most common type of corporation is an LLC. Because most small and medium-sized businesses are best organized as a corporation or Limited Liability Companies, this article focuses on the fundamental similarities and differences. I attempted to provide a synopsis of the following key elements. However, keep in mind that the following information will not allow you to make an informed decision about a person. This can all be accomplished with the help of a lawyer and an accountant.

C Corporation

The largest firms are C firms. C Companies are all publicly traded companies. The term "C" is taken from the Internal Revenue Code, Subchapter C, which controls corporate taxes. There are some reasons why C businesses are more appropriate for large firms. Multiple stock groups, infinite number and shareholder forms, a fiscal year versus a calendar tax year, and corporate profit retention are just some of the major differences of a C Company. This is generally ideal for companies that want publicly to raise capital or whose class of investors differs.

Most notably, double taxation extends to C Companies. This means that all of the profits of the C Company are once taxed at the corporate level, and then the same income is taxed again at the shareholder level when the benefit is a dividend. Double taxation can sometimes be avoided in smaller C Companies by annually abolishing net profits by paying shareholder workers. Shareholders must declare any dividend earnings as capital gains on their tax returns.

For tax purposes, a business begins as a C Business. Unless the shareholder elects "S" corporate tax status, as discussed below, all companies will be known as C Corporations by default. The corporation's net profits (after deducting pay, company expenses, and furniture and equipment depreciation) are net. The C Corporation will only be taxed on "effectively related" revenue from a corporate tax rate of 15% on the first $50,000 taxable income per year.

When the organization is listed as a "Personal Service Business" (PSC), a flat fee of 35 percent from the dollar of a net profit would be charged. This is a typically unwanted form of entity. The CSPs are companies whose owners operate in accounting, acting, architectural, technological, health and veterinary services, law, and performance services. The lowest tax rate of 15 percent is only possible for a business that offers personal services if the company does not employ and hold at least 6 percent of its issued stock. Otherwise, the highest personal tax rate will apply to personal service taxable income in that business. A PSC is, by definition, a C organization. A timely S-election will negate your Company's classification as a PSC and escape the 35% flat tax rate.

The use of a C Corporation results in some special tax advantages. One of the most significant advantages for SMEs is the ability to deduct all health insurance premiums paid by employed owners and their spouses and dependents. Furthermore, a C Corporation may enact a MERP (medical, dental, and drug expenses refund plan) at any time during the fiscal year, which can be easily applied back to the beginning of the fiscal year, and can purchase disability insurance for one or more of its managers or other workers. An organization can also exclude disability insurance premiums without affecting the executive's or employee's taxable expenses. Finally, contributions to eligible pension programs will be deducted by an employer.

In terms of ownership, the company is held by shareholders under the company's ownership of stock (or shares). Corporations issue their shareholders' stock certificates to show their ownership percentage. C Companies can have different asset groups, such as common and preferred stocks, offering shareholders different dividends and voting rights. Without affecting the company, shares can be freely exchanged or redeemed. According to Illinois law, like every other Jurisdiction, corporate shareholders typically have a full liability shield from the actions or omissions of the company. The shareholders elect a board of directors who oversee the company's operations and businesses. The law of Illinois requires the appointment of a President, Secretary, and Treasurer, while sole shareholder companies are allowed.

The corporation's bylaws are its guiding text. The bylaws regulate the business and affairs of the company (C and S Companies) and define the board of directors amounts, powers, and obligations, the shareholder's voting rights, the company's dissolution, annual meetings, special meetings, and other corporation rules. Generally, a stock buying/stock restraint contract or similar agreement regulates the relationship between the owners (shareholders) of a small or closely held company. This instrument can provide for buying and selling rights of shareholders, restrictions on the sale or transfer of shares, and purchase rights for companies, among other items. Corporations shall have a collection of bylaws regulating the company in all jurisdictions, or the corporation shall be subject to the default rules set out in the State statute.

Notice that the corporation owners (shareholders) arrangement may also be subject to a separate instrument, such as an inventory purchase or an agreement on inventory restriction, shareholder agreement, or similar document. In general, this document governs the transfer and acquisition of stocks, companies, and/or shareholders.

C Corporation is ideally suited to active companies with a chance of appreciating and high share potential. C businesses typically keep their profits in the early stages of growth and do not share corporate income with shareholders to enjoy it.

S Corporation

S Corporation is a lot like C Company. Its owners are similarly shielded from personal responsibility for the actions or omissions of the companies.

The key difference lies in the S corporation's tax treatment. As suggested, C Companies are taxable at the corporate level, and shareholders are taxed from the same revenue stream as paid as dividends. S Companies, by comparison, prevent dual taxation since only individual owners are taxed. The status of a company is achieved by electing such organizational tax treatment (IRS Form 2553). Net profit, including wages paid to workers and shareholder-employees, after expenses incurred for S companies is declared in federal Form 1120S and transferred to shareholders' tax return through Schedule K-1, where the return is subject to the regular tax. In addition, pass-through losses are restricted to the taxpayer's basis in the S Company stock.

All salaries are taxed on self-employment (payroll). S Companies shall pay shareholder-employee fair wages in exchange for the services the employee gives to the company before non-wage distribution to the shareholder-employee can be made. The S Company pays the employer's share of FICA tax (7.65%), and the employee pays the balance of the FICA tax (7.65%). For the S Company and the shareholder, salaries are subject to a cumulative payroll tax of approximately 15.3 percent plus the shareholder's income tax rate. So, the shareholder-employee can only pay a minimum wage to himself to minimize taxes on the profit stream of businesses. IRS regulations specify that the shareholder-employee be paid fair compensation (many consider this failure to cause an internal audit). However, any other income avoids self-employment taxation and is either subject to ordinary income or capital gains. This means that payroll taxes can only be levied on the fair salaries of employee-holders, not the distributions of the S business.

When do you have to pay salaries? According to the IRS, the shareholder-employee shall assess fair compensation for the S Company. The IRS shall investigate the source of the gross receipts of the S Company:

1. Shareholder services.
2. Non-shareholder staff services.
3. Capital and equipment.

If the gross receipts and income are obtained from things 2 and 3, the shareholder-employee shall be paid no compensation. However, if the bulk of gross sales and income are related to the shareholder's services, part of the profit allocation should be distributed as compensation. (Of course, you can seek more information from an accountant).

Individual owners can still be charged even if profits are not allocated to the owners and are left as working capital. This is because all revenue is distributed directly to shareholders. C-corporation owners are only liable for the dividend taxes they currently collect (although the corporation's undistributed revenue is exempt from self-employment tax).

The disadvantages of the S election position are that the S Company holders to whom they pay the deductions on life benefits, disability insurance, car and life, drug, and dental insurance plans will be taxable.

S Corporations, among other things, are less adaptable than C Corporations and LLCs. Only a few shareholders are allowed; individuals and no foreign shareholders are usually permitted. Small and closely-held businesses that do not intend to publicly raise large sums of capital are generally better suited in this context. In the case of a C venture, the shareholders own the company through their stock in the company. However, unlike a C Corporation, there can only be one type of distribution rights stock.

Corporations typically have low debt, low risk, and a low chance of major appreciation for active companies, as all corporate profits normally are allocated to shareholders.

Limited Liability Company (LLC)

An LLC provides the same personal liability shield that a company offers to its shareholders. However, it offers great flexibility in dealing with capital contributions and allocating gains and losses to shareholders. An LLC will allocate income as it sees fit for its members. For example, assume that you and your partner have an LLC to which you contributed $80,000 of capital and only $20,000 from your partner. If your partner works 80%, the owners will still decide to share the 50/50 profits. However, if you and your partner were shareholders in an S firm, you would have to allocate 80% and 20% to your partner under the statute. If you have any partners, this can be an unfair way to organize your company.

The LLC is taxed as a partnership, as gains and expenses are passed on to the members, and no income tax is charged at the corporate level. The LLC prohibits double taxation, much as the S business does. (Again, some states levy LLC income substitution taxes). The income of the LLC is shown in Form 1065, then distributed via Schedule K-1 to the owners. The owners then record their income (1040) on Schedule E. If the LLC has only one owner, then the IRS considers the LLC automatically as a single owner ("unregarded entity"). A neglected individual does not file a tax return, and the owner declares the profits in compliance with Schedule C of its return. The IRS will immediately handle the LLC as though it were a partnership if the LLC has multiple owners. However, an LLC is a 'check the box' company, which means it may choose to be taxed as a corporation.

There is a lot of misunderstanding regarding self-employment taxes for LLC members. The disparity in your treatment as a general partner and a limited partner, in general, is important in the calculation of self-employment tax liability since an LLC is taxed as a partnership. If a member of an LLC is regarded as a limited partner, the member's share of LLC profits does not have a self-employment tax (except for all guaranteed payments). If a Member is a general partner, they must pay tax on all LLC incomes for self-employment. However, under Section 11402(a)-2 of 1997 Proposed IRS Treasury Regulations, if an LLC member has the authority or provides more than 500 hours per year of service to an LLC of being directly liable for any debt, that member shall, as the general partner, be taxed and shall have a self-employment tax duty on his LLC revenue allocation. Otherwise, the member will be charged as a limited partner and does not have tax responsibilities relating to its LLC revenue allocations for self-employment.

The LLC may also have two interest groups, one of which is treated as a general partnership interest and one as a limited partner interest. If a spouse or member owns both classes of interest, the member may divide the income share between the two classes and pay self-employment taxes on the general partner side but not the restricted partner side. The IRS never formally enforced the draft Regulations for 1997, but many practitioners and taxpayers relied on them. Furthermore, IRS officials have now confirmed that they can rely on it.

Both benefits and losses allocated to members and "salaries" (usually guaranteed payments) paid to them shall be called independent jobs and subject to self-employment taxes. LLC owners are deemed self-employed and must pay a 15.3 percent self-employment fee. Note that only wages are subject to job taxes and not distributions to shareholders in an S Company. The S Company thus gives its shareholders substantial job tax benefits compared to the LLC.

LLCs provide limited liability insurance if properly formed and maintained in most cases, but there are typically few tax advantages to the corporate partnership over the sole proprietorship. The ability of members to limit the transfer of a membership interest to only economic interest is a significant advantage of LLCs over corporations. This means prospective members will only collect dividends (and pay taxes) but have no voting or management rights. If a business shareholder transfers its stock, all ownership attributes, including voting rights, must be transferred unless the stock is non-voting.

The owners of LLCs are called shareholders, and each member has an interest in the business as a percentage of the LLC. LLCs can establish different groups of membership interests similar to C corporations. Members include companies and other LLCs, which provide this organization with ultimate flexibility in its ownership structure. An LLC is typically operated by its members, where the LLC's company and operations are operated by its members themselves, or where either a Member Manager or a foreign manager is named. Members commonly control LLCs. Illinois provides one-member LLCs, like most other nations, if not all. Unlike several other jurisdictions, Illinois requires licensed service providers, such as lawyers and physicians, to create LLCs for business operations.

The Operating Agreement serves as the LLC's guiding document. It is the same as corporate regulation in effectively regulating the same aspects. Most jurisdictions, however, state the contents required in bylaws and operating agreements, and there are, of course, differences. The operating agreement frequently specifies the relationship between the members of an LLC. At the same time, companies typically use various instruments for some shareholder rights, such as stock transfer and buy-out rights of companies.

Real estate investments and companies holding other properties that typically expose their owners to liability risks are generally suitable for LLCs. If you have one or more partners and want flexibility in how the organization distributes benefits (and losses) to its members, the LLC is likely to be the right option.

CHAPTER 5

WHAT CAN A LIMITED LIABILITY COMPANY OFFER TO A SMALL BUSINESS?

COMPANIES THAT PROFIT FROM THE LLC STRUCTURE

In general, LLCs are best suited for:

Organizations with few active shareholders. When there are no more than about 35 owners, the practicalities of making joint choices on the company's direction may be easily managed.

New small businesses. New enterprises typically want to pass on early-year losses to shareholders to deduct against other revenue (Typically, salary obtained while working for another firm or investment income).

Whoever is considering establishing an S-Corporation. S companies, like LLCs, provide all owners with limited liability protection and allow income and losses to be taxed at individual shareholder rates. However, as we'll see in "S corporations," these advantages come at a steep cost: S companies are extremely restricted, and a company might lose eligibility inadvertently—for example, when an ineligible shareholder inherits or purchases shares or when the number of shareholders exceeds the maximum allowed—resulting in large tax payment.

Partnerships that already exist. Only the LLC allows for partnership-style pass-through taxation of business profits while shielding all owners (rather than just limited partners in a limited partnership) from personal liability for corporate obligations.

Real estate holding businesses. When assets are sold or liquidated, C corporations with their shareholders are subject to a double tax on appreciation—taxation happens at both the corporate and individual levels. S corporations that were formed as C corporations may be liable to double taxation on gains from valued assets and a penalty tax on passive income (money from rents, royalties, interest, or dividends) if it exceeds a certain threshold. Because the LLC is a real pass-through tax form, it permits a company to avoid double taxes on appreciated assets. When a firm is sold, the proprietors, not the entity, often pay taxes on the sale gains.

INCORPORATING SUCCESS IN YOUR BUSINESS

Setting up a Limited Liability Company or LLC is one of the best options for you as you build the business side of your hotshot company. Forming an LLC gives you several advantages and safety nets as a business owner.

It shields you from personal liability and establishes a limited liability structure through the business. You will also be given a Federal Employer Identification Number, which functions similarly to a social security number for your company. If you want to open a bank account or conduct business with your state government, this will be required.

You are not required to file a corporate tax return; however, you will be required to file with your state. Creating a Limited Liability Company also gives you financial options such as a business, including lines of credit, loans, and business rate credit cards. These are based upon your Federal EIN and the credit you build through your Company.

Laws and fees vary by state, and you aren't even required to open the LLC in the state you reside or operate in. However, you are required to have a registered agent in that state.

You can form an LLC on your own by submitting paperwork to your state, but it is strongly recommended that you hire an attorney or a registration company to handle the paperwork. A lawyer will be more expensive than a registration company, so the final decision is yours. However, once your Limited Liability Company is formed, you must follow up with your state government regarding any additional fees or documents that must be filed.

Often, businesses will form an LLC in a state with lower taxes or fees, but you must have a physical address and someone working for you in that state. Many LLC registration companies will provide the registered agent, including it in the first-year filing fee.

Liability Protection

The LLC creates a shield for small business owners. These are not directly responsible for the company's debts and commitments. This legal entity also offers a single taxation layer that minimizes taxes on shareholders and allows active members to deduct from other incomes if the Company generates losses.

They are a popular business structure for small businesses because they offer flexibility, limited liability protection, and the possibility of a lower tax bill. This entity operates as a corporation in the state but is taxed like a partnership or sole proprietorship in the federal government. It provides its owners with the same limited liability protection as a corporation while avoiding double taxation by passing earnings through to the owners. When Limited Liability Company members pay their income taxes, they are taxed only once.

There are no restrictions on how many members it can have. These businesses do not require a board of directors or even multiple members. You can form a single-member LLC.

The process of forming one is straightforward. You can hire an agent to do it for you or apply at the state secretary's office. You'll have to pick a business name and file your articles of organization. This document is the governing rulebook for your Limited Liability Company. In the case of single-member LLCs, it isn't particularly important. However, you should have a lawyer draft this agreement with multiple members since it can have massive implications for your revenue split and other operational questions.

Along with your articles, you'll need to draft an operating agreement that details how you and your partners will run the LLC daily. One of the members is usually designated as the managing member and is in charge of the organization's operations. Many states do not require operating agreements, but it is a good idea to create one anyway in case of future disputes.

LLCs can hire employees; to do this; you'll need to apply for an EIN with the IRS. Once your agreement and articles have been filed with the state, some states will require you to post an ad in the newspaper announcing the formation of your Limited Liability Company. You'll have to check which publications are appropriate for this with the local county office.

Raising money is simple with an LLC, unlike sole props, even if it isn't as easy as a corporation. An investor becomes a member, not a shareholder since they can't issue shares themselves. While membership is a good option for new investors, it can get tricky to cash their money out (Zarzycki, 2020). I'll address this situation shortly.

The most appealing aspect of an LLC is that it protects its owners from liability while also allowing you to reduce your overall tax bill. When establishing one, you must open a separate bank account to hold the Company's funds. If you do not do this, you may expose your assets to liability litigation. In some states, if it is operated from your bank account, it is used as evidence that your assets are also involved in the litigation, and the LLC's protection is voided.

Income is not the end of security and taxes. The Limited Liability Company also allows business owners to change how they want to run and manage their company. You are not required to fit into a standard size that applies to all governance systems.

Business owners frequently build their companies without holding legal persons or complying with legal enforcement criteria. The legislation governing limited liability companies was specifically designed to encourage the use of this vehicle. A minimum requirement is the formation and management of a Limited Liability Company.

Another advantage is that a lawyer's corporation conveys a more professional and official profile. Customers understand that the company is a Limited Liability Company and that its founders took their work seriously. It's great to do more business.

So, when we ask what LLC stands for, we get the most common small business legal entity vehicle. A business owner receives numerous benefits and advantages in exchange for a low price.

Excellent Defense from Lawsuits

These business organizations can also protect a business owner from someone who wants to prosecute him. If you properly sign as management or a mere member, the organization can help you against any lawsuits. This likewise means that you do not insert your expenses into your company account and are running your bank account as a company. The courts will investigate how you independently run the company, which means they will check if the corporation is on its own two feet and has its accounts and expenses independent from the employees. If you have not deferred the company reports, you would be well-positioned to protect yourself from liability. This also means you have not committed fraud, as these institutions cannot defend you against fraud if you face a trial. If the opposing party demonstrates fraud, it quickly becomes the corporate veil.

LLC Taxation

Certainly, the LLC tax is distinct from corporate tax. The LLC S business policy helps reduce the self-employment tax or fully avoid it. You have all the usual business tax write-offs open to you. However, if you work solely under the corporate agency for your Company, you cannot escape a self-employment tax. You can look for an accountant and understand a corporate structure to mitigate self-employment tax.

An example of this is an S Company which pays you to form your Limited Liability Company. There is a lot of Limited Liability Company information about Internet taxes that you can find. Different tactics shift year by year; what appeals most to business owners to the concept of avoiding self-employment tax. Becoming an employee of your own company is the most sought technique.

Furthermore, your LLC pays for the establishment of a business. Paying a low income and thus paying large dividends reduces net tax even further. These techniques can be complex and necessitate extensive research and good CPA implementation.

It's fine to start operating with your LLC and earning more than an accountant in the early stages of your business. Forming a corporation at the state level is usually more expensive and necessitates more laws and regulations to ensure enforcement and corporate custody.

Profits, losses, deductions, and credits all pass through to your income, and you must include them all on your tax return at the end of the year. In addition, your LLC will be required to pay state income taxes and other business-related taxes, such as self-employment taxes. It is best to have them filed by an accountant.

CHAPTER 6

COMMON MISTAKES TO AVOID WHEN FORMING AN LLC

O perating a small business is a challenging experience for even the most seasoned small business owners. Mistakes are common in business, so it is critical to learn from your mistakes. However, it is also beneficial to avoid making the same mistake. This chapter will address some of the most common LLC mistakes to help and guide you when forming and operating an LLC.

One of the most common mistakes is filing to become an LLC in the wrong state. Your geographic location may prevent you from any other option, but it needs to be considered. Some states have a better relationship with their LLC owners and treat them better than other states. This is also true for other business operations within the state.

It is recommended that you conduct some research before filing to form your LLC to determine whether your state has any strict or flexible business statutes. At the very least, this research will give you an idea of what your company is in for in the long run. The history of how your state treats small business owners will help you understand how current fees will change over time and what the tax obligation will look like in the future.

You should probably just file in your state if you're just starting a small LLC because all states value small business owners, some advantages that companies that do not incorporate will not have.

Not following through and understanding your company's legal obligations to conduct business in your state is a huge misstep. It is a common misconception that incorporating your business gives it legitimacy in the community.

Every business will still be required to obtain and maintain current business licenses for the community they operate. Depending on the nature of your business and the products or services you offer, you will need to obtain a business license or license to comply with local and state laws.

After you have become an official LLC and obtained all of your business licenses, there is the task of remaining an LLC in your state. Every state will have requirements you and your LLC must meet to comply with the LLC rules and regulations.

If you do not maintain your compliance as an LLC, you risk jeopardizing the protections for which you formed your LLC in the first place. If your safeguards are compromised, your assets may be vulnerable to litigation, and you may lose your business and personal financial stability.

There are several ways to stay compliant to protect your personal and business assets. The first is one in which many business owners struggle. Keep your funds separate from those used solely for your business.

Because there will be no co-mingling of accounts or funds, keeping your funds separate protects your assets by not allowing your funds to be accessed in litigation.

Another common blunder is failing to use your company name when signing business documents. Using your business title complicates the argument that your signature was done personally. The main reason for forming an LLC is to protect your assets from litigation, so keeping your company business and personal business separate will eliminate the appearance of conflict.

Follow all of your state's requirements to stay in compliance with the state and protect yourself and your company from losing the status of protection that comes with operating an LLC. Your state will require you to submit an annual report detailing your income and any legal actions you have taken.

These annual reports must be submitted by a specific deadline, and you must ensure that you meet those deadlines. You must file for foreign qualifications if you are filing from a different state. To avoid losing your in-compliance status, ensure that you meet the state's requirements in which you are filing.

To ensure that your company remains in compliance, you must stay up to date on any changes made in your state or the state where you file your paperwork to ensure that you have met all of the requirements. These modifications may impact the deadlines and due dates for various aspects of an LLC's formation and certification process.

One of the most common misconceptions among business owners is that an LLC will protect its company in any situation. While incorporating your company into an LLC will provide you with significant protection, it will not protect your company at all costs. If your company engages in unethical or illegal behavior, it may breach the security provided.

Finally, the most common mistake made by a small business owner is assuming that your Company is too small to effectively form an LLC or Corporation to protect any of the Company or your assets.

If you pay attention to current trends, you will notice that it is very common to file lawsuits to the right that may only be perceived as wrong by one customer. It is extremely prudent to keep your personal and business finances separate.

Assume you decide not to incorporate your company and instead run it as a sole proprietorship. In that case, you will jeopardize all of your assets and expose yourself and your partner's assets to litigation. You will most likely be working more than 80 hours per week to generate new business to make your business as successful as possible. However, you will need to devote some time to incorporating or forming an LLC.

You will then be able to modify the structure of your business in a much more effective and efficient way in the future.

| MISTAKES TO AVOID WHEN SETTING UP OR ENLISTING

For decades, an LLC has been a reliable way to protect your assets from the liabilities associated with apartment rental property. State governments provide this defense to encourage investment, strengthen the economy, and benefit society.

Fortunately, one of the primary purposes of Company and LLC laws is to protect private investors from personal responsibility to support society and the general public. However, a business must operate following the LLC statutes to receive the security shield. People frequently make serious mistakes when setting up their LLC or enlisting the assistance of a discount legal document service, a paralegal, an accountant, or even an attorney who is not specialized in LLC preparation. (Although a tax accountant's services are of considerable value, they are generally not carried out from an asset security point of view).

1. Wait before a tenant claims an injury or has started civil proceedings against you. If the LLC does not exist until a tenant claims or takes legal action, you gain zero insurance for your assets if you then make the LLC. It never ceases to confuse me how many consumers panic and hurry to create an LLC after being sued. It's always too late at that point.
2. Suppose the rental property is not transferred to the LLC properly when the LLC is formed. An LLC provides its owners with asset security only when the LLC transfers and retains the underlying rental property. A major step is to use a Quitclaim Deed or Grant Deed, which must be carefully worded and legally notarized. Unfortunately, many people did this critical process independently instead of relying on a paralegal or document preparation service. Errors or omissions will result in an unintentional and unnecessary reassessment of property tax in any detail if not done correctly. A reassessment caused by a previous customer who wanted to move his property without proper instructions can be very costly to reverse. In retrospect, the authors of these errors probably wished they had hired an experienced LLC lawyer from the start.

3. If the LLC bank account is not opened, all LLC businesses operate from this account. While some of my new customers have formed an LLC, all LLC banking transactions have been handled through their accounts or DBA. All LLC revenue must be deposited into the LLC account, and all LLC expenses paid from the LLC account must be reimbursed. If a lawsuit fails to distinguish LLC funds from personal funds, the LLC will be disqualified, allowing creditors to threaten and seize personal property. Rent checks must be made payable to the LLC and deposited in the LLC account. All costs, including but not limited to mortgage payments, insurance, taxes, and maintenance, must be covered by the LLC account. You can pay an LLC cost regularly with your own money and then write an LLC check to repay yourself in an emergency. This, however, can be kept to a bare minimum. In addition, your LLC should be equipped with a credit/debit card for small property transactions. If you use an agency to collect rentals in your name, the agency must forward rental income to the LLC rather than to you directly.

4. Shape a business rather than build an LLC for your rental property. To save money, many people make the mistake of forming a company for their rental property without seeking legal advice. This is a bad idea because a company like an LLC does not always protect this type of business. Extra tax filings and formalities, such as required meetings and business minutes, are frequently included in corporations. Even if you later decide to be taxed as a business, you can request that the IRS treat your LLC as an S or C corporation by filing the appropriate forms. I've had several clients who paid a paralegal or legal document service to help them set up an LLC or a company. They only discovered significant issues later and sought legal aid as a result. They are deeply dissatisfied because they have paid a lot of money for worthless or incorrect papers and franchise taxes and started from scratch.

5. If you have a Living Trust, you must ensure that your LLC becomes or is owned by your trust. I met several new customers who had not transferred their LLCs into a family trust. If they died before the matter was settled, the LLC and its assets would be scrutinized and not directed toward the heirs, as the trust is designed to do. This is another area where competent legal counsel is essential to ensure that your properties are protected from legal action, well-maintained, and not subject to probate or excessive property taxes. Many other mistakes can be avoided by hiring an experienced LLC lawyer. If you have decided to form an LLC, it is not

prudent to ensure that it is properly formed and operated. The LLC is a legal entity. However, improper use jeopardizes the safeguards it can provide.

| CHAPTER 7 |

BENEFITS OF LLC FOR PROPERTY OWNERS

One of the most difficult aspects of starting a real estate investment business, whether a partnership or a sole proprietorship, is how to structure it. It is important to protect yourself from personal liability by separating your finances from your professional life. In most cases, it is nice to consult a real estate lawyer to review the different options and determine which one is right for you. In California, an "S" corporation or LLC may be better suited to your corporation because they are "pass-thru" tax entities in which individual shareholders pay a personal income tax. A "C" corporation may require more complex organizations, a separate taxable entity. In both cases, a real estate lawyer can help you in this decision-making process.

Suppose you're going to run your business as a sole proprietorship. In that case, you don't legally need a business plan like you do if you're going to invest in a Limited Liability Company, but I would urge you to have one anyway. The difference between a sole proprietorship and LLC is that a Limited Liability Company is an established business in the government's eyes. It can be costly to start. However, it comes with several benefits, the biggest of which are the tax benefits and the protection it provides you in the case of a lawsuit. I urge you to look into getting an LLC rather than running your business as a sole proprietor.

A business plan is a document where you write down your business goals, how you intend to achieve them, and how long it will take you. A business plan also describes your company's nature, financial projections, and the steps you intend to take to achieve those projected goals.

It's important to have a business plan because it lays out your goals and the strategies you'll use to achieve them. Remember, you're laying out a strategy for success. You can effectively sit and spin your wheels until you run your business into the ground if you don't know your goals and how to get there. You are more likely to succeed if you have a clear action plan.

At the very least, it should include:

- A current budget.
- A three-year sales forecast.
- Sales and production strategy.
- Market analysis.
- Projected expense budget for three years connected to your current budget.
- A profit and loss statement.
- Break-even analysis
- Team outline (strengths and how to deal with their weaknesses/ manage them).
- SWOT (strengths, weaknesses, opportunities, and threats relating to your business).
- Product and/or services summary.
- Mission statement.
- Vision statement.

If you're writing up a plan for people to invest in your company, you'll also need an income projection. It's not necessary, however, if the plan is just for yourself.

When developing your plan, consider how much money you need to make to reach certain business milestones, where you are now, and how you will get from where you are to where you want to be. You will also need to determine the best way to reach your target market. There are numerous marketing strategies to choose from; you must be astute in determining which strategy is most effective for your target market. It is also beneficial to cultivate relationships with other small business owners to contract when you need work done.

Every business is different. The approaches to selling products and services differ depending on what kind of business you have. And those approaches will also differ per product or service. You need a strategy for each, and your business plan is the way to achieve that.

You may have different divisions that fall under the umbrella of your brand. It is normal to use a different marketing strategy for each division. For example, you may have a home renovation aspect to your brand and the investment division. The marketing strategies you will use to attract renovation projects differ from your strategy for expanding your investment portfolio.

REAL ESTATE TAX STRATEGIES AND FORMING AN LLC

If you plan to travel from New York City to San Francisco, you will see good road signs that will help you find your way without needing a detailed road map.

The same applies when you decide to invest in the business. If you have a clear picture of the benefits and advantages of different kinds of real estate deals, assess your current position in terms of resources, and move in the right direction with the least amount of wasted time, it will be a major asset to you. This chapter's goal is to help you see where you are, where you want to go, and the best way to get there.

The first thing you should do is go over your current financial evaluation. Is your credit good or bad? Do you have access to money lending avenues? Are private and public lenders ready to help you get started?

Once you have examined your current status, you are ready to start selecting the right kind of deals to push you towards financial freedom. For instance, if you have smaller credit resources, you will want to select real estate deals that do not depend on credit or funding.

PROPERTY TYPES AND INVESTMENT APPROACHES

Real estate investing is a great option because there are so many different types of properties to invest in and techniques for what to do with those properties. And each has its own set of benefits.

Investors weigh various options based on the outcome they want to achieve, the amount of money they want to put into the project, and their level of experience with various strategies.

For example, an investor may prefer quick cash investment methods for various reasons, such as a lack of working capital or high consumer debt.

Multiple income streams and opportunities necessitate specialized knowledge in various areas.

Multiple Income Streams

You could be wondering how to select your income streams and what factors should dictate your decision. Here's a list of the different types of income:

- Wholesaling.
- Probate.
- Remodeling.
- Rehabbing.
- Land development.
- Discount note selling.
- Foreclosures.
- Meanwhile, here are some passive streams of income in real estate:
- Leases.
- Property management.
- Recreational parks.
- Rentals.
- Apartment houses.
- Mobile home parks.

In general, anything you will contract and sell quickly falls into earned income.

Passive income refers to money that you get week after week or monthly without going out and making/closing another deal. As a result, passive income is sometimes called a recurring income.

For real estate, properties that fall under passive income streams are your buy-and-hold rentals. Once you close on these deals, you collect rent every single month. Another real estate field that can be considered passive is when you become a property manager or own a property management company. Investors use you to collect the rents and pay you some fee for doing it.

PORTFOLIO INCOME

Here is when your money starts to generate more money for you, especially through interest.

There are different ways to generate portfolio income that is real estate related. Most of these income methods relate to investors earning interest on their money.

Types of Streams of Portfolio Income in Real Estate

Real estate can help investors build wealth in a systematic, compounding manner.

While everyone is different and has different time demands and goals, professional real estate investors will always want to have 3-5 streams of earned income and 2-3 streams of portfolio income.

New investors with a limited amount of money start by being knowledgeable in various earned income streams like foreclosure, wholesale, and rehabbing. They now have a lot of control over their ability to generate large sums of money in a short time. They then take that money and begin investing in real estate, buying, and holding.

As the passive income or lease option properties grow, the investor has two options: buy another buy and hold property or invest in a portfolio stream.

Distressed Properties vs. Motivated Sellers

An old saying about real estate investing goes, "There are only two types of deals out there, distressed properties or distressed sellers."

You will realize that certain properties have a higher ideal investment opportunity than others, no matter your investment strategy. Professional investors evaluate each deal against a set of criteria, considering the benefits of that type of deal versus the opportunities available. They do not always exhibit all the characteristics listed, but they assess and make well-informed decisions.

When evaluating a distressed property, look for the following advantages:

- They have minimal competition because the average individual wants properties in the best condition.
- You can always buy distressed properties under flexible, easy terms and prices relatively below the market value.
- You have the freedom to heighten the value through smaller improvements and rehab work.
- A lot of market areas have many distressed properties to select from.

Some things to consider about distressed properties include:

1. Many real estate markets have a certain number of investors searching for this type of property, so your marketing efforts should be active, well-organized, and effective to discover better deals. It can be great to investigate different marketing strategies well for other real estate investors.
2. To avoid costly mistakes, you must know how to examine the property and neighborhood accurately.
3. Through inspections and repairs, estimates have to be done before the purchase.
4. If the property is in a low-income neighborhood, comparable sales in that area will exceed a certain amount of money, regardless of how the change is made. Repairs are usually expensive. To maximize profitability in older, lower-income areas, it is safe to combine a distressed property with a distressed seller and maximize profit potential in all aspects.

Meanwhile, here are the pros of working with distressed sellers:

- In each price range, there is seller distress. Property can sometimes be purchased in flexible and simple terms. The seller requires assistance and, in most cases, simply wants a way out but is unsure what to do. You can provide a solution.
- When you can connect a distressed seller with a distressed property, you have a great opportunity to increase property value through cosmetic changes.

You must determine what caused the seller's situation and the best way to assist them in escaping it. You must develop good listening and negotiation skills to understand their problem and find the best solution.

Certain distressed sellers provide compelling reasons for wanting to stay in their properties, which tends to accommodate this. This can be risky if their problem is financial. It is important to keep your emotions at bay.

Purchasing as Wholesale

Distressed properties are the best option for wholesaling candidates, and wholesaling is a great opportunity because it requires the least expertise and is the kind of deal new investors want.

Because you have a good chance of finding distressed properties, wholesale deals may be one of the first types of deals you make in real estate investing.

To be successful in wholesaling, you must understand how to segment your market correctly, create a database of potential properties, and many other things. You must also understand a few fundamental aspects of the wholesale business, such as:

1. Analyzing Prospects

Because distressed properties should be your main target, you must learn to identify and review distressed homes. You should also understand that a distressed property does not necessarily imply a good deal but rather a great starting point. As a result, you must memorize the techniques that will assist you in determining when a deal is too good to be true, when it is appropriate to proceed, and when the deal should be abandoned.

2. Computing the Market Value

To succeed as a wholesaler, you must know the significance of calculating fair market value after repairs. The real estate experts on your power team will be valuable assets for finding this information. Also, using comparable sales of properties in the same location will allow you to know the market value.

3. Estimating Repairs

This will not work if you do not accurately estimate repairs. Learn how to check deals to ensure that you present an offer that will result in the greatest profit. You can also learn techniques to help you save money on rehab projects while increasing your profits.

4. Submitting Offers and Counteroffers

You have to become familiar with good communication and negotiating skills, learn how to submit offers and counteroffers without destroying your goals, and learn how to manage contracts. Understanding how to review properties properly will be significant in determining what to offer and whether you need to make an offer.

5. Getting Buyers

Wholesaling is only half done when you find deals and bargains but have no one to assign contracts to. Creating a large investor database to tap into, regardless of the type of deal you're working on, will help you move things along quickly while maintaining your profit margins.

HOW TO CLOSE EFFECTIVELY

You must learn the right ways to close without money.

Lease Options

Leases are one of the most appealing real estate investment opportunities for both new and experienced investors because they can generate multiple income streams from a single transaction. Here are some general points you need to know about lease options in real estate; if you purchase a property using a lease option, you can:

- Engage with distressed sellers rather than distressed properties. The seller's circumstances create the deal. What you must do is identify the owner's issues.
- Acquire freedom of a property without taking ownership. You are not required to buy, but you have earned the right to do so.
- Manage beautiful homes in beautiful settings. In this case, the seller must exit, and the investor must enter. Demand rises as the neighborhood improves.
- Help someone in a variety of ways. The most distinguishing feature of lease options is always debt relief. You are constantly dealing with people who do not want to sell their property but are forced due to financial constraints. Thus, you can help someone find a solution quickly. Likewise, you can do it with or without money.

Foreclosures

The foreclosure market can be a great channel for making a profit for new and experienced investors. Foreclosures occur daily, and this could be your opportunity to make a wise investment and assist someone in need.

Keep in mind that foreclosures can happen for various reasons, and this is a niche where you can achieve a win-win scenario and do something that assists both you and the individual in need. Investors must negotiate well with lenders and homeowners to boost profits on these deals.

With so many different strategies and ways to make money in real estate, knowledge will be essential for success.

You will have completed your first critical step toward financial independence by reviewing the available opportunities in real estate investing. It's time to move on to the next level.

CONCLUSION

Limited Liability Companies are popular due to the elements that allow the corporation and the partnership to work together. For example, when signing up for an LLC, you eliminate some of the negatives of being a Corporation or a Partnership alone. The LLC will provide limited liability to the owners and the shareholders and offers a pass-through income tax rate.

The benefits can be more advantageous because it provides more flexibility to business owners, resulting in an agreement for operating based on the owners' needs and requirements. It provides limited liability for the members or shareholders by holding the company liable for its debts and liabilities. It benefits the LLC because it is not taxed at the corporate level. Instead, it permits the Company's losses on their returns to be passed on to individual shareholders. Finally, it assists the Company in avoiding double taxation, allowing them to keep profits within the Company for future growth.

However, there are several disadvantages to the LLC. One of those disadvantages is the pass-through tax status. The losses and profits are reported on the individual's tax returns, which can be unfavorable if the shareholders receive some dividends. Due to the LLC structure, the investors may be hesitant to invest or loan money to the company. You also may find that you have more taxes or fees associated with the LLC. There is a required upfront cost in some states that initially costs higher. These states require the LLC to pay a franchise or capital values tax, often based on revenue, owners, and profitability.

S CORPORATIONS FOR BEGINNERS 2024

The Most Updated Guide on Starting, Growing, and
Running your S Corporation and Save on Taxes
as a Small Business Owner

THOMAS NEWTON

INTRODUCTION

An S Corporation, otherwise called an S subchapter, is a type of corporation that adheres to particular Internal Revenue Code regulations. Without paying federal corporate taxes, it may distribute income to shareholders (along with other deductions, credits, and losses). The S Corporation status, typically associated with small businesses (those with fewer than 100 shareholders), effectively provides a business with the benefits of incorporation while retaining the tax-exempt status of a partnership.

This makes an S Corporation, which is so-called because it must pay taxes under Subchapter S of the Internal Revenue Code, an advantageous option for many business organizations, especially small businesses. While it comes with a few limitations, such as rigid requirements, the advantages of S Corporation certainly outweigh the disadvantages for small-medium organizations.

However, it is a completely alien subject to many people outside the business world. Besides, the concept can sometimes seem complicated to laymen and young entrepreneurs, as they often find the pieces of information about S Corporations somewhat inaccessible. Even when you surf the web for information on S Corporation, what is obtainable leaves much to be desired. This book aims to address this gap by providing an updated guide on how to start, and grow, your S Corporation. If you are a small-medium entrepreneur planning a startup in Texas or any other place in the US, this book was intended for you.

The book dissects S Corporation from its skin down to the bone marrow. In other words, it provides a background to the subject, including a comprehensive definition of the concept as well as its benefits and disadvantages. Perhaps you have been wondering whether an S corporation rather than a C Corporation is for you or otherwise. You have probably been wondering how you can save money through S Corporation. Also, you have imagined whether it is worth the hype. With this book, you are going to become better armed to make an informed decision.

You will learn about other types of companies, their pros and cons, and how they differ from S Corporations. The details in this chapter will be useful to people who are just considering going into business and are undecided about the type of company that is best for them.

If you have made up your mind about forming an S Corporation, Chapter 8 is one useful topic you will find indispensable. It is right in the heart of the book. It highlights the S Corporation's mistakes and ways through which you can avoid them. You may need to take the time to read this chapter many times over.

Because S Corporation has a lot to do with taxes and taxation, this book will help you improve your knowledge of taxation. For example, it provides useful details about how tax deductions and credits affect your business tax rate. It also shows how you can handle your business taxes without making mistakes that can lead to conflict with the government. Best of all, you get the benefit of learning about tax breaks and deduction tactics as a small business.

I have decided to make my writing as easy to read as possible, albeit the technicalities surrounding the subject. This book is a guide that endeavors to achieve its aim through two methods. First, the majority of the contents are exposition in nature, revealing everything about S Corporation. Secondly, the book provides a step-by-step guide on how anyone can set up S Corporation without any glitches.

As such, I have attempted to break down complex topics using easily digestible language. The presentation of the topics and ideas was not designed for business gurus. Rather it aims to help small business owners in their journey towards succeeding and becoming gurus in the nearest possible future.

In short, S Corporations can be a powerful tax planning tool for small businesses. The benefits include the elimination of self-employment tax and the elimination of corporate income tax. This brief book discusses everything you need to know about S Corporations, especially how they can create value for your small business. I hope you find this book helpful and that it will help you make an informed decision. Let's get started!

| CHAPTER 1 |

EXPLANATION OF S CORPORATIONS

| WHAT IS S CORPORATION?

S Corporations are a popular choice for privately held small and medium-sized businesses. This structure is more difficult to set up than private companies or partnerships, and it frequently necessitates the assistance of a lawyer and an accountant. This raises the associated costs, both in terms of development and maintenance. One option for lowering compliance costs is first to form an LLC (which we will discuss shortly) and then elect S Corporation tax status. The best thing about an S Corporation is that you must pay yourself a reasonable salary (which is subject to FICA tax) as the owner. Nonetheless, the remainder of the company's profits is subject only to income tax, not FICA tax.

S Corporations are held to higher standards than other types of companies. In general, you must be an individual to own an S Corporation (and a U.S. resident or citizen). This is a barrier for companies seeking corporate or foreign investors (e.g., start-ups seeking venture capital funding). Although trusts and estates can own S Corporations, partnerships and corporations cannot. Profits and distributions are also rigid: they must always be allocated according to ownership.

Losses may be restricted in their use. In some cases, an S Corporation owner with losses may be unable to deduct them on their tax return. This would be carried forward to the following year, but most new businesses would welcome the extra cash from a tax refund now, not later! Such losses are usually easier to claim as a partnership or sole proprietorship.

One benefit of incorporating as an S Corp is reduced self-employment taxes. This taxable entity status has two components: salary and distribution. The self-employment tax applies to only one component of an S Corp: salary. Lower self-employment taxes may assist you in lowering your overall tax liability. Consider sole proprietorships, partnerships, and limited liability corporations as alternatives. In these cases, the business's total net income triggers self-employment taxes. Because of this, whether you keep the profits or not, you still have to pay self-employment taxes.

The second benefit is that the distributions to shareholders or owners are not taxed. An S Corp can provide significant tax savings because it can distinguish between salary and distribution components of income. If you intend to use this division to reduce your taxes, a good rule is to withdraw approximately 60% of your company's net income as salary; otherwise, the IRS may investigate your company for potential tax evasion.

This business entity can also live independently. What does this mean exactly? Well, other business types are connected to the death or exit of the owners from the business. On the other hand, an S Corp is independent of its owners. It will survive whether the owners stay, leave, or die. Due to its independence, it is an ideal business structure for long-term growth and longevity.

The third benefit of establishing an S Corp is liability protection. In certain circumstances, you will never be personally liable for your company's debts. When another type of business entity fails, the creditors or claimants of that entity have no recourse against your assets.

The fourth advantage is ownership transfer. If you leave the company, you will find it much easier to transfer your ownership than with other business entities. You can take one of two approaches. The first option is to sell your stock outright, in which ownership is immediately transferred to the buyer in exchange for monetary considerations. The second method of transferring ownership is a gradual sale. This option entails selling your stock in the company over a set period. Consider it like a payment or amortization schedule. Whatever option you choose, the entire ownership transfer process must be formalized with a printed and signed sales agreement.

The last advantage of forming an S Corp is credibility. Because this business entity is well-known among many prospective investors, customers, and vendors, forming an S Corp may provide your company with increased market credibility.

However, while an S Corporation may be the best business structure for certain purposes and the best entity solution for particular business concerns, there are some limitations to be aware of. These include:

- Restrictions on S Corporation ownership eligibility and shareholder number.
- More than 100 shareholders are not permitted in an S Corporation.
- Non-US residents are not permitted to be shareholders in an S Corporation.

Other corporate legal entities, such as C Corporations, LLCs, LPs, and certain trusts, are not permitted to be S Corporation shareholders. However, bankruptcy estates, death estates, and certain tax-exempt organizations may own S Corporation shares.

- **Restriction on the stock class of an S Corporation**: Furthermore, an S Corporation may have no more than one class of stock.
- **Restriction on an S Corporation's ability to choose its tax year:** Except for a few exceptions, an S Corporation must generally use a calendar year as its tax year. A calendar tax year is 12 consecutive months beginning January 1 and ending December 31.

Additional Compliance Requirements for Employee Payments

An S Corporation may pay its shareholder-employees a reasonable salary and periodic distributions. The S Corporation, on the other hand, pays payroll taxes on employee salaries. As a result, S Corporations will sometimes disguise them as corporate distributions to avoid paying payroll taxes on employee salaries. In response, the IRS thoroughly investigates how S Corporations pay their employees (particularly shareholder-employees).

As a result, to discourage and prevent employee salaries from being disguised as distributions in S Corporations, the IRS has enacted the following compliance rules:

1. The salary must be fair.
2. A reasonable salary must be paid before any distributions are made.
3. Even distributions (profits and losses) to S Corporation shareholders must be allocated based on each shareholder's percentage ownership of the S Corporation.

Based on the preceding, an S Corporation faces a high risk of IRS audit due to the IRS's interest in discouraging, preventing, and penalizing the compliance mentioned above.

The S Status of an S Corporation is not indefinite. The IRS has the authority to terminate it for a cause.

Another significant limitation of the S Corporation is that the S Status (basically, flow-through taxation) can be lost if even one shareholder transfers their S Corporation shares to an owner who is not legally permitted to own shares in an S Corporation (e.g., transfers the S Corporation's to a non-US resident). If the S Corporation status is lost, the S Corporation reverts to a regular C Corporation and is taxed from that point forward. Furthermore, the now-reverted C Corporation will be barred from filing another S Corporation election for the next five years.

- S Corporations, like C Corporations, must be registered with the state and are more costly to form.
- Administrative duties are required; S Corporations are subject to more restrictions on stock issuance than C Corporations.
- Estates, individuals, and trustees are the only types of stockholders.
- The company cannot offer paid fringe benefits; it is expensive to establish and has ongoing expenses such as franchise tax fees.

- Unlike other business entities, you must be a legal resident of the United States.
- Ownership is limited because there can't be more than 100 shareholders.

Annual shareholder meetings are one example of a corporate formality to consider.

The IRS Form 2553 must be submitted when converting your company to an S Corporation. It could be beneficial for a company that needs a corporate structure with tax flexibility similar to that of a sole proprietorship. All states do not recognize it; it is only valid within the United States.

| CHAPTER 2 |

IS AN S CORPORATION THE CORRECT DECISION FOR ME?

D eciding to form an S Corporation will benefit you in various ways, most of which have been discussed in the previous chapter.

While avoiding self-employment tax may sound appealing, shareholders in an S Corporation must pay themselves reasonable compensation, subject to Social Security and Medicare taxes. What exactly is adequate remuneration? In general, you would compute that based on several factors.

The taxation process is the only distinction between a C Corporation and an S Corporation. While a C Corporation is subject to double taxation (corporate tax and personal income tax on shareholders), an S Corporation is subject to pass-through taxation, which means that profits and losses are passed through to the owners' tax returns. S Corporations must file their taxes annually, whereas C Corporations must file quarterly.

An S Corporation can enjoy tax benefits similar to a traditional corporation while avoiding disadvantages. You must meet IRS requirements and have no more than 100 shareholders to qualify for S Corporation status. S Corporations must also pay a yearly fee based on their revenue. S Corporations are easier to acquire than traditional corporations because partners can own them. The main advantage of an S Corporation is that it can benefit from a corporate income tax reduction. Revenue can be taxed individually and treated as a partnership, making this a viable option for assisting small businesses in growing and receiving income.

| THE OPERATING AGREEMENT FOR AN S CORPORATION

As hinted earlier, to elect to be taxed as an S Corporation, the entity must file Form 2553. (Election by a Small Business Corporation). The timing of this election is where things get a little complicated. Small business corporations must make the election either during the previous taxable year or before the 15th day of the third month of any taxable year.

When an entity chooses S Corporation status, it keeps it until the election is revoked. When an entity chooses S Corporation status, it keeps it until the election is revoked. At least one-half of the corporation's shareholders must agree to the S termination Corporation's methods:

- The revocation is retroactive to the first day of the corporation's tax year if made by the 15th day of the third month.
- If made after the 15th day of the third month, the revocation takes effect on the first day of the following tax year.
- The corporation revokes the election by filing a statement stating that it has done so.

This is where things get tricky. The Small Business Act of 1996 authorized the Internal Revenue Service for the first time to grant relief to entities that filed an election after the deadline. If the Service determines that there was reasonable cause for the failure to hold a timely election, the S election will be valid. This was a significant change in S Corporation law.

There are three ways to seek relief for submitting a late S election today. The first option is for the corporation to seek relief under Rev. Proc. Rev. Proc. 2007-62 2003-43 if it can show that it had good reason for failing to make a timely S election and meet certain deadlines. Assume the IRS fails to notify a corporation of a problem within six months of the due date for filing a timely S Corporation return for the first year the corporation intended to be an S Corporation. In that case, the corporation may file a request for relief under Rev. Proc. 97-48. The third method of requesting relief is through a private letter ruling.

Suppose the corporation's stock is issued to a nonresident alien, a non-qualified trust, another corporation, a partnership, more than the permitted shareholders, or more than one class of stock. In that case, the S election is statutorily revocable. Furthermore, the election can be revoked if the corporation's passive investment income exceeds 25% of gross receipts for three years.

Relief for an S Corporation that unintentionally revokes its election by failing to meet the requirements of a small business corporation or failing the passive income test. If the Service determines that the termination was made inadvertently, steps were taken to correct the cause within a reasonable time of discovery, and the corporation and each shareholder agree to the Service's adjustments, the Service may grant relief.

S Corporations can be challenging to comprehend. The important point to remember is that once you've made your decision, it must be carefully monitored by a professional. To obtain S Corporation status, a company must meet specific IRS requirements. Among these qualifications are the following:

- Being incorporated domestically (within the U.S.).
- Shareholders who meet certain eligibility criteria.
- Have only one type of stock.
- A maximum of one hundred shareholders.

Individuals, specific estates and trusts, and tax-exempt organizations (501(c)(3) are all eligible to be S corporation shareholders. Corporations, partnerships, and non-resident aliens are not permitted to participate as shareholders.

HOW TO APPLY TO BECOME AN S CORPORATION

- Enter your company name and address.
- Enter your business's EIN. We obtained your employer identification number (EIN) from the IRS. It's a 9-digit number.
- Enter the Date Incorporated as the date on your company's charter.
- Input the state of incorporation. It is the state in which your business is registered.
- Enter your first, last, and job title.
- Enter your phone number here.
- Enter your first and last name, as well as your street address.
- Date and sign
- Check the entire form for accuracy before printing.
- Fill in your title, date, and signature.

You've completed your task. The IRS will review your request and send you a letter indicating whether it is approved. The letter of determination should arrive within 60 days. If you haven't received the letter within 60 days, you can call the IRS at 1-800-829-4933 to find out where it is. Once you receive the IRS determination letter stating that your company is approved to be treated as an S Corporation, it is officially an S Corporation. You can pay salaries, run payroll, file S Corporation tax, etc.

| CHAPTER 3 |

DIFFERENCE BETWEEN S CORPORATIONS AND OTHER TYPES OF COMPANY

Deciding on the right business structure is crucial to the success of all businesses. The previous chapters provided an in-depth exposition on S Corporation, highlighting the advantages and disadvantages and other important things small business owners should know. You have also been exposed to the requirements for starting an S Corporation. However, it is not the ultimate business structure. It is instructive for every entrepreneur to ruminate on the business structure that serves their interest best. This chapter examines other types of businesses in relation to an S Corporation. The expositions presented on these types of companies will help to highlight how each differs from S Corporation. Let's start with Sole Proprietorship.

SOLE PROPRIETORSHIP

This means that a single person will manage your company. This is a popular option for small businesses. Although it is a simple and low-cost business structure, it increases your liability and costs you significant tax benefits.

With this structure, you cannot pay yourself a salary. Instead, you will withdraw profits as needed. Every year, whether you have withdrawn the profits, you must pay personal income tax on the entire taxable profits of the company.

Remember that most benefits are subject to federal income tax and Social Security and Medicare taxes (or "FICA"). Many small business owners pay FICA taxes in addition to income taxes.

Sole proprietorships are intended for small, single-owned businesses (small service businesses, food stands, freelancers, consultants, etc.)

Because sole proprietors lack stock or ownership units, the only way to exit is to sell the company's assets.

Pros of Sole Proprietorship

- It is simple to get started because there is no registration required.
- Decisions can be made quickly because there is no need for consultation.
- No double taxation exists because the business and the owner are treated as one entity; thus, business income is reported on a personal income tax return.
- Only the income generated by the business is taxed.
- If the business makes a profit, the owner gets to keep it because they are the sole proprietor.

Cons of Sole Proprietorship

- Unlimited liability means that if the company cannot pay its debts and liabilities, the owner's assets, such as your car or home, can be used to make the difference.
- Social Security and Medicare taxes are double what you would pay as an employee.
- If the company suffers losses, the owner is solely responsible.
- Because there is no separation between you and the business, obtaining a business loan from a lender is difficult.

Most startups are sole proprietorships due to the ease with which they can be established. Unfortunately, unlimited liability exists because there is no separation between the owner and the business, which can be extremely dangerous. As a result, most of these businesses convert to LLCs or corporations.

Sole Proprietorship versus S Corporation in a nutshell: The major difference between Sole Proprietorship and S Corporation is that the latter has the privilege of limited liability protection while the former does not. Also, the business owner of an S Corporation pays income tax and FICA on their "reasonable salary" and only income taxes on distributions, while his counterpart in a sole proprietorship pays income taxes on the net profit of the business and self-employment taxes.

| PARTNERSHIP

A partnership is like a sole proprietorship in that it has multiple owners. In most cases, extraordinarily little (or no) paperwork is required to establish and maintain a partnership.

Because of this, many small businesses are formed as partnerships. Although the paperwork requirements are minimal, multi-owner companies are inherently more complicated, so at least one partnership operating agreement that governs the business's operations and ownership is strongly recommended.

Only in the case of partnerships is it not necessary to allocate the firm's income proportionally to ownership. This flexibility can be beneficial when a silent partner has contributed most of the capital but does not expect a comparable share of the profits. A partnership agreement should clearly state any such arrangement.

In short, this structure is commonly used by small, new businesses that have yet to achieve true profitability. This is particularly relevant for small businesses with no employees, where the owners do most of the work (perhaps in your case?)

While the structure is advantageous, there are liability risks. You are equally liable for your partner's mistakes because of how a partnership is structured. Many partnerships fail because they form with people close to them and cannot handle disagreements. As a result, you should proceed with caution before forming a partnership.

A general partnership is simple to establish. There is no need to file any forms. All that is required is a verbal agreement. However, recording your agreement in a legal document is a good idea. In a legal dispute, this partnership agreement will prevent many problems.

Partnership Agreements

The partnership agreements function like the bylaws of a corporation. Here's what the agreement should establish:

- The name of your partnership.
- How profits and responsibilities will be shared.
- How losses will be shared.
- The terms of exiting and entering the partnership.
- The different sections of the agreement need to describe the following items at a minimum:
- The nature of your business.
- The partnership's establishment date and its expiry date.
- The duties that every partner will be expected to undertake.
- The amount of capital and resources each partner will contribute to the partnership.
- The rules of dissolution of the partnership.

How will disagreements be resolved along with the proper procedure and documentation?

A lawyer should handle all partnership-related paperwork. Because each business has unique requirements, it is best to tailor the agreement to your specific needs. The most significant advantage of forming a partnership is that it is less formal than forming a corporation or a limited liability partnership (LLP).

As with sole proprietorships, all partnership income is considered personal, so you must only pay taxes once. This could result in a lower tax bill than forming a corporation would. However, there are some significant drawbacks to consider.

I've already mentioned how you'll be held accountable for the mistakes of others. However, it is not only incorrect but also indebted. If your business partner makes a bad decision and borrows more money than your partnership can afford, your creditors will not distinguish between you and your partner; you're both equally liable.

A partnership is not the best business structure for a freight brokerage. It may be more practical for you to incorporate as a sole prop and collaborate with your partner, who may also incorporate as a sole prop (if forming a corporation together is not an option).

Pros of Partnership

- **Easy to start** – It's easy to start since it doesn't require registration. If the business incurs losses, it's divided by the partners, and the burden is shared.
- **Less capital required** – All the partners contribute towards raising the capital rather than raising it alone.
- **Consultation** – There must be consultation among the partners if a decision needs to be made, ensuring they make the best decision.
- **Less business loss** - The business losses can be deducted from the partner's tax returns.
- **No double taxation** – the business and owners are viewed as one; hence the business income is reported on each partner's income tax return.

Cons of Partnership

- **Unlimited liability** – The partners remain liable for the business debts and liabilities. If the business cannot repay its debts, the partners' assets can be used to settle the debts.
- **Issues between partners** - Disputes among the partners could negatively affect the business.
- **Partner liability** - In some states, the partners are liable for each other's careless behavior.

- **Hard to get loans** - Obtaining loans for a business that lacks registration is difficult.

Startups form partnerships primarily to reduce the risks associated with starting a business independently. They provide an excellent support system, but you should be cautious about who you partner with.

Partnership versus S Corporation in a nutshell: A partnership does not require the partners to do any paperwork with the government or fill any form. On the other hand, the formation of an S Corporation is a lot more complex, with specific requirements spelled out. The main steps you will need to take to apply for an S Corporation have been highlighted in the previous chapter. In addition, the structure of an S corporation is not as flexible as a partnership. In terms of key decision-making, for instance, all partners in a partnership have an equal say in every business decision. However, a board is elected in an S Corporation, enjoying the privilege of voting for or against any major business issues.

C CORPORATIONS

Because the C Corporation structure is generally preferred for complex and large businesses, it will not be your first choice. These are the country's largest corporations, accounting for roughly half of all business profits in the United States despite accounting for only about 5% of all businesses.

Let's review its main characteristics to understand how it differs from other business types.

C Corporations comprise all large publicly traded companies in the United States. Private C Corporations are unusual and are typically formed for reasons other than taxation. One company that uses the C Corporation structure is a high-growth start-up seeking serial financing. They are compelled to take this route because their intended investors may be foreign entities or individuals who cannot invest in an S Corporation. The main difference between C Corporations is that they pay income taxes.

The main disadvantage of this structure is that C Corporation shareholders must usually pay taxes on corporate dividends. So, first and foremost, the C Corporation is required to pay income taxes. The remaining funds are then distributed to the owners, who must again pay taxes. This is referred to as double taxation.

This double taxation discourages private companies from using the C Corporation structure. What about another disadvantage? Losses from a C Corporation cannot be deducted from a stockholder's other personal income.

Pros of C Corporations

- The owners, who are the shareholders, are not liable for the Corporation's debts and liabilities.
- Corporations are entitled to more tax breaks than other types of business entities.
- Corporations can raise more capital by selling stock on the stock market.
- A Corporation's ownership is easily transferable, which means that if the owners believe the business will fail, they can sell it without losing their capital investment.
- Employees benefit from not paying taxes on health insurance premiums and life insurance, which are fully deductible as corporate expenses.

Cons of C Corporations

- A corporation is more expensive to establish than other types of business entities.

- Double taxation exists because the corporation and the shareholder's income are taxed on dividends.
- When forming a corporation, a lot of paperwork is involved, including legal paperwork that must be filed with the Secretary of State.
- The shareholders have no say in how the corporation operates.
- Because the directors must be consulted, decision-making takes time.
- Losses incurred by the business cannot be deducted from the owners' tax returns.
- Many corporate formalities exist, such as shareholder meetings and by-laws.

Because of the complexities involved, most startups do not choose to form a corporation, but as your business grows, it provides more legal protections.

C Corporation versus S Corporation in a nutshell:

Both C Corporation and S Corporation derive their names from the Internal Revenue Code under which they are taxed. S Corporations are taxed under Subchapter S, while C Corporations are taxed under the Subchapter C of the IRS Code. Taxation is the major yardstick for drawing a difference between these two entities. While an S Corporation enjoys pass-through taxation, a C Corporation is a separately taxed entity. Nonetheless, the different entities can be differentiated by considering shareholders' restrictions. While C Corporations do not have shareholder restrictions, an S Corporation cannot have more than 100 shareholders.

LIMITED LIABILITY COMPANY (LLC)

The IRS does not recognize an LLC as a taxpaying business structure; instead, it is a legal entity only. This means that the owners of an LLC must choose one of the other structures discussed above as their tax identity.

At the same time, LLC structures have additional advantages. Limited Liability Companies, for example, help protect the owner's assets from a business lawsuit, in contrast to sole proprietorships and partnerships. Without an LLC, a sole proprietor or partner may become personally liable for a lawsuit or judgment that exceeds the business's assets, potentially exposing the owner's assets to a claim. A "limited liability" corporation cannot do this.

What else is there to say? In general, the structure of an LLC is simpler to manage than an S or C Corporation. True corporations, for example, are required to hold annual meetings and keep minutes of those meetings. An LLC taxed as a corporation is typically exempt from these rules.

Furthermore, a company that starts as an LLC has the option of changing its entity later on. So, once your business is profitable, you can form an LLC taxed as a partnership and then convert to an S Corporation.

Most of the time, the LLC umbrella does not affect taxes. An LLC owner must decide whether the business should be a C or S Corporation, a sole proprietorship, or a partnership for tax purposes.

LLCs are a popular business structure for small businesses because they provide flexibility, limited liability protection, and a potentially lower tax bill. This entity operates in the state like a corporation but is taxed by the federal government like a partnership or sole proprietorship. It offers its owners the same limited liability protection as a corporation while avoiding double taxation by passing earnings through to them. When members of an LLC file their income tax returns, they are taxed only once.

Because LLCs are formed at the state level, the laws governing their formation differ. There are no limitations on the number of members an LLC can have. These companies don't need a board of directors or even multiple members. A single-member LLC can be formed.

The procedure for forming an LLC is straightforward. You can hire an agent or apply directly to the state secretary's office. You must register your company and file your articles of incorporation. This document serves as the operating manual for your LLC. In the case of single-member LLCs, it isn't particularly important. If you have more than one member, you should have a lawyer draft this agreement because it can significantly impact your revenue split and other operational issues.

Along with your articles, you must draft an operating agreement outlining how you and your partners will run the LLC daily. One of the members is usually designated as the managing member and oversees the LLC's operations. Although many states do not require operating agreements, drafting one is a good idea in case of future disagreements is a good idea.

LLCs can hire employees, but they must first obtain an EIN from the IRS. Some states will require you to place an ad in the newspaper announcing the formation of your

LLC after you have filed your agreement and articles with the state. Check with your county office to see which publications are appropriate for this.

Unlike sole proprietorships, raising funds with an LLC is simple, though not as simple as with a corporation. Due to the inability of LLCs to issue shares, an investor becomes a member rather than a shareholder. While membership is a good option for new investors, cashing out the money can be difficult (Zarzycki, 2020). I'll get to this right away.

An LLC's most appealing feature is that it protects its owners from liability while also allowing you to reduce your overall tax bill. When forming an LLC, you should open a separate bank account to hold the company's funds. If you do not do this, you may expose your assets to liability litigation. If you operate the LLC from your personal bank account, it can be used as evidence that your assets are also involved in the litigation, and the LLC's protection is null and void.

Pros of LLC

The tax advantages of forming an LLC do not end with single taxation. You can file as a C or S Corporation if filing as an LLC does not result in a lower tax bill. Your LLC will be required to pay corporate taxes in this case. LLCs are extremely adaptable, with every aspect of their operation customizable to meet your specific needs. Whether it's a change in how profits are distributed to members or a change in the operating agreement, you can do it all with little effort.

If you have employees, you can elect to be taxed as an S corporation to avoid paying self-employment taxes. Therefore, limited liability companies (LLCs) are popular among freight brokers. They are ideal for a beginner because they provide the flexibility and credibility you need to present to your clients.

- Limited liability means that the owners are not personally liable for the debts or liabilities of the company.
- Members can instruct the IRS on whether their LLC should be taxed as a partnership or corporation.
- Establishing an LLC is simple because it only requires filing with the Secretary of State.
- Members are not personally liable for their fellow members' irresponsible behavior.
- There is no double taxation because it is imposed on the personal or corporate level, but not both.

Cons of LLC

LLCs have a few drawbacks. The most significant disadvantage is how a departing member is treated. Assume an investor wishes to withdraw funds; dealing with this situation can be challenging. The member's shares would be purchased in the case of a corporation but not in the case of an LLC. Many states require the LLC to be dissolved, whereas others permit the departing member to be bought out.

LLCs are taxed in some states, which can be costly for some businesses. For example, a minimum tax of $300 per year is required in Delaware, regardless of whether the business makes a profit. Some investors are hesitant to invest in LLCs because of the issues with member exits.

Despite these disadvantages, LLCs are ideal for individuals who want to start a new business and eventually grow into a larger corporation. While running a corporation can be expensive, LLCs offer cost savings and all the protection you need to run your business safely.

- An LLC is more expensive to establish than a sole proprietorship or general partnership.
- Because they have unlimited liability, partners in charge of operations are liable for any debt incurred by the business.
- Any disagreements among partners are likely to have an impact on the business.

Small businesses generally prefer the limitation of Liability Companies because they combine the legal protection of corporations with sole proprietorships or partnerships.

Limited Liability Company (LLC) versus S Corporation in a nutshell: Limited Liability Company (LLC) is often discussed in the same context as an S Corporation. Therefore, many people confuse the two as options that can be chosen one against the other. However, each of them refers to separate aspects of a business. While an S Corporation is essentially a tax clarification, an LLC is a kind of business entity or a legal business structure just like a partnership or corporation. Put differently, an S Corporation is registered as either an LLC or as a C Corporation as part of its requirements.

LIMITED PARTNERSHIP

Limited partnership business entities must register with the state, which entails filing paperwork. There are two kinds of partners in a Limited Partnership:

1. **General Partners**: The general partners own the company, run it, and bear its liabilities.
2. **Limited Partners**: Limited partners are investors who are not involved in the business's day-to-day operations. They are also known as silent partners because their liability is limited to their capital contribution.

The following are the advantages and disadvantages of forming a Limited Partnership:

Pros of Limited Partnership

- The general partners can obtain the funds required for the business while continuing to operate.
- A limited partnership is a different way to raise funds from investors without personal liability.
- The partnership must not be dissolved if a limited partner wishes to leave.

Cons of Limited Partnership

- If limited partners become unintentionally involved in business operations, they may face personal liability.
- A Limited Partnership is more expensive to form than a General Partnership.
- General partners are personally liable for the debts and liabilities of the company.
- Limited Partnerships benefit business owners with multiple businesses because they can bring in investors with limited liability.

| CHAPTER 4 |

HOW YOU CAN SAVE MONEY WITH S CORPORATIONS

S Corporations, like partnerships, are required to report their deductions and income. S Corporations must file annual information returns (Form the 1120S) to report their income, profits, deductions, losses, and tax credits. Schedule K-1 must be provided to shareholders by S Corporation owners detailing their ownership interests in the items listed on their 1120S. Stakeholders use Schedule E and individual income tax returns (Form 1040) to report their share of the corporation's loss of income.

S Corporations are distinguished from partnerships by the employment status of the company's owners. A partnership-taxed LLC's owner is not considered a worker of the LLC. They are merely a business proprietor.

On the other hand, an S Corporation employer who performs more than minor functions for the corporation is taxed as both an employee and an owner. In effect, the owner of such a corporation typically wears two hats: shareholder (owner) and employee.

Employees and self-employed people pay the same Medicare and Social Security taxes, but they are paid differently. The employer withholds half of the total tax and deducts the other half from the employee's pay. It makes no difference if the employer pays half or not if you own a business that pays these taxes—you are the employer.

The owner/employees' efforts must be rewarded with a fair wage and any other employee benefits desired by the corporation. The employee/owner must report the S Corporation's earnings on their tax returns and pay their share of Medicare and Social Security taxes on all employee salaries. On behalf of the owner/employee, the corporation should withhold and pay federal income taxes, employment taxes, state and federal unemployment taxes, Social Security taxes, and Medicare.

SAVINGS ON EMPLOYMENT TAXES

Being classified as an S Corporation employee has several significant advantages. If you use the S Corporation tax procedure, you may be able to withdraw funds from your business without incurring employment taxes. This is because you are exempt from paying employment taxes on the corporation's distributions. That is, you, the owner, pay taxes on income passed through your corporation rather than being paid as an employee for your work. The lower the employment tax, the higher the distribution. S Corporations are the only business structures that allow owners to defer Medicare and Social Security taxes. This has historically been the primary reason for S Corporations' popularity.

You would owe no Medicare or Social Security taxes if you did not receive any pay. According to the IRS, S Corporation employees and shareholders must be paid a reasonable wage comparable to what comparable businesses pay for comparable services. Furthermore, an S Corporation may find it advantageous to pay large employee salaries due to pass-through tax deductions.

TAX DEDUCTION FOR PASS-THROUGH

The Tax Cuts and Jobs Act added new deductions for pass-through corporations, which include sole proprietorships, partnerships, limited liability companies, and S Corporations. Owners of these entities have been deducting approximately 20% of their income from their taxable income since 2018. This is the personal deduction that all pass-through entity owners can claim, regardless of whether they itemize.

TAX-FREE WEALTH

Tax-free investing is a great way to avoid looming tax increases. You can defer paying taxes on a portion of your income and assets. Aside from S Corporations, here are some other tax-advantaged strategies to consider adding to your portfolio or expanding your use if you already have them.

CAPITAL GAINS ON LONG-TERM INVESTMENTS

Long-term capital gains are typically taxed at a maximum rate of 20%. Many people are unaware that the 20% tax rate only applies to those with the highest incomes. Lower income levels have lower rates. For many people, such capital gains are taxed at 0%. And the figure is less than 10% for many others. Qualified dividends should be taxed the same as ordinary dividends.

Qualified dividends and gains on sales of assets held for more than a year are taxed at 0% until they exceed the threshold amounts if taxable income other than long-term profits or dividends does not exceed $40,400 for a single taxpayer, $54,100 for household heads, or $80,800 for joint filers.

While capital gains and dividends are not taxed at the federal level, they increase adjusted gross income, which may result in higher taxes on Social Security benefits and other taxes. Furthermore, capital gains may be taxed differently in your state.

You can avoid paying taxes on long-term capital gains by managing your taxable income.

Avoid actions that will increase your gross income, such as increasing traditional IRA or 401(k) distributions. Instead, if possible, take additional distributions from tax-free accounts. If there is no urgent need to sell investments this year, you can do so next year.

You can also consider increasing your deductions and lowering your taxable income. For example, charitable contributions from multiple years can be combined into one year when itemized expenses are deducted.

Another possibility is to liquidate investments in which you have incurred paper losses. This loss is deducted from the year's capital gains. Losses more than gains of up to $3,000 may be deducted from other revenue, and any excess losses may be carried forward and used in the same manner in subsequent years.

Remember that to qualify for long-term capital gains, an asset must be held for more than a year. A one-day early asset sale results in a short-term gain taxed as regular income.

529 COLLEGE SAVINGS PLANS

These savings plans are excellent estate planning tools because they provide tax-free investment returns. You contribute to the 529 plan and select a beneficiary. A child or even a grandchild is typically named beneficiary, with the expectation that the account will be used to fund a child's college education in the future.

You can use up to five years' worth of the $15,000 annual gift tax exclusion in a single year when contributing to the account. This ensures that a gift of nearly $75,000 is exempt from all gift taxes and does not deplete your lifetime estate or gift tax exclusions.

▎INDIVIDUAL HEALTH SAVINGS ACCOUNTS

These are the three-tiered tax strategies available, and they are an excellent way to save for retirement. Many high-deductible medical insurance policies and plans allow the insured to contribute to health savings accounts (HSAs).

Contributions are tax deductible when made personally and are tax-deductible when made by an employer up to a certain annual limit. The account can be used to make investments, and earnings accumulate tax-free.

HSA distributions are tax-free if they are used to pay or reimburse you for qualified medical expenses that are not covered by other sources. In addition, if you had unreimbursed medical expenses in previous years, the HSA may be able to reimburse you tax-free.

Every eligible person can open an HSA and contribute the maximum amount allowed annually. You must contribute if your employer does not contribute to the annual cap. Transferring funds from a taxable cash account to an HSA makes sense.

QUALIFIED SMALL BUSINESS STOCKS

A worthwhile investment in a small business may be tax-free up to a certain amount. A qualified small business is organized as a "C" Corporation in the United States of America. Sole proprietorships, S Corporations, and limited liability companies are not permitted.

Stock must have been issued after August 10, 1993 and acquired explicitly from the corporation in exchange for cash, property (other than stocks), or services. Additionally, the overall tax basis of the business's total gross assets must be less than $50 million when the stock is received.

401(K)S AND ROTH IRAS

Transferring assets to ROTH accounts creates a long period of tax-free earnings and gains. Contributions to ROTH accounts continue to have no tax advantages. The advantages include tax-free investment returns and tax-free distributions of accumulated funds.

ROTH IRA and ROTH 401(k) contributions are permitted (k). You can also convert a traditional IRA or 401(k) to a ROTH IRA.

LIFE INSURANCE

Life insurance benefits are possibly the longest-lasting tax-free asset, and their status is unlikely to change anytime soon.

Throughout your life, you can borrow tax-free from the cash value account of most perpetual life insurance policies and the benefits payable to beneficiaries. Nonetheless, any unpaid loans reduce the number of benefits payable to beneficiaries.

Asset repositioning as life insurance might be a good idea. You could, for example, withdraw funds from a traditional IRA and then use the after-tax proceeds to purchase permanent life insurance or establish a trust for your children or grandchildren.

The guaranteed life insurance benefit will be tax-free to the beneficiaries. The life insurance gain will exceed the IRA's after-tax value for many people. It is also not subject to market fluctuations, unlike an IRA.

Other assets could be restructured as life insurance, providing beneficiaries with tax-free inheritances. Health insurance can be purchased through the marketplace and deducted as a business expense for your S Corporation. You must adhere to specific rules and regulations. If you have high-deductible health insurance, your S Corporation can contribute to your HSA as part of your employer contribution. Consult your tax advisor for more information.

CHAPTER 5

HOW TO SET UP YOUR S CORPORATION

PRIMARY CHARACTERISTICS OF AN S CORPORATION

The S Corporation as a Separate Legal Entity

The S Corporation is a legal entity in and of itself. Its existence is distinct from that of its shareholders. It has its name, identity, personality, rights, and responsibilities. It also has its own IRS taxpayer account number (EIN). In short, an S Corporation is a separate legal person with all the rights and responsibilities.

The S Limited Corporation's Liability Provision

S Corporations, like C Corporations, benefit from limited liability protection. This feature (if properly implemented and enforced) will generally protect the S-shareholders Corporation from personal liability and their assets from seizure due to the S-debts Corporations and liabilities. Who can form an S Corporation and/or own shares in one?

One or more shareholders typically form an S Corporation, but no more than 100 shareholders are permitted.

In addition, S Corporations can be formed or owned by US citizens and residents. Non-US resident aliens, on the other hand, are not permitted to be shareholders in an S Corporation.

Shares of an S Corporation may also be owned by bankruptcy estates, death estates, and certain tax-exempt organizations. However, corporate legal entities (such as LLCs, C Corporations, LPs, and certain trusts) are generally not permitted to be shareholders of an S Corporation.

It is important to note that the secondary sale of an S Corporation by an eligible shareholder to a non-eligible shareholder may void the status of the S Corporation, converting it to a regular C Corporation. If this occurs, the now-reverted C Corporation cannot file another S-status election for five years.

| HOW AN S CORPORATION IS FORMED

In this case, the application would essentially be for forming a regular corporation (a C Corporation). A C Corporation is "born" after the Articles of Incorporation are approved. In other words, an S Corporation is formed from a C Corporation. Following that (and if eligible), the C Corporation may file IRS Form 2553 to elect to be taxed as an S Corporation. The C Corporation becomes an S Corporation after 2553 is approved.

The Governance Document for an S Corporation

As with the C Corporation, corporate bylaws (which should be custom-drafted) provide and govern the rights and responsibilities of the S-shareholders, corporation's directors, and officers. The corporate bylaws establish the general guidelines for the S-internal corporation's operations. If the S Corporation fails to have and maintain corporate bylaws, it may lose its limited liability protection and become subject to the state's default corporate rules.

Meetings, Minutes, and Resolutions of the S Corporation

S Corporations, like C-corporations, are required by law to hold an annual shareholders' meeting because they are corporations. Corporations (including S Corporations) must hold regular board of directors and shareholder meetings. Meeting minutes and any resolutions reached during such meetings must be documented and kept as part of the S-business corporation's records.

THE MANAGEMENT STRUCTURE OF AN S CORPORATION

The management structure of an S Corporation is similar to that of a C-corporation in that a board of directors and officers manages it. The shareholders of an S Corporation elect the board of directors to oversee the corporation. The directors also appoint the officers who oversee the day-to-day operations of the S Corporation. A single shareholder can serve as the corporation's sole director and officer in a single-shareholder S Corporation (or C-corporation) (where allowed under state law).

The Reliance of S Corporations on Corporate Formalities

The directors and officers of an S Corporation must also treat the S Corporation as a separate, distinct, and independent legal entity and thus must adhere to corporate formalities. Again, suppose the corporation's officers, directors, and shareholders fail to have, keep, and comply with corporate bylaws. In that case, the S Corporation will most likely lose its limited liability protection feature (thus exposing the shareholders, directors, officers, and their assets to risk). The S Corporation may also become subject to the state's default corporate rules.

As you can see, the S Corporation provides two of the most important and desired features in a business structure: limited liability protection and flow-through taxation. However, the S Corporation has numerous shareholder restrictions (such as no nonresident shareholders; generally, no corporate entity shareholders; and no more than 100 shareholders, etc.).

To make matters worse, an S Corporation may lose its S-status due to a shareholder-eligibility violation. If it does, it may not file another S-status election for five years.

In short, the limited liability company (LLC) was legislatively accepted and introduced in the United States in part to address and amend the limitations mentioned above. As a result, the LLC has more expansive and inclusive ownership/shareholder eligibility standards (which the S Corporation does not have), and the two most-desired S Corporation features limited liability protection and flow-through taxation.

Employee Fringe Benefits and the S Corporation

An S Corporation may provide pre-tax health insurance to its employees. It may also offer health insurance to its employee-shareholders (S Corporation shareholders who are also S Corporation employees). The health insurance premiums the S Corporation pays its shareholders are deductible business expenses. It also counts as income for the individual shareholder. Furthermore, an S Corporation does not provide a medical-reimbursement plan to cover its employees' additional medical expenses.

PRIVACY AND S CORPORATION

It is possible to structure a corporation (including an S Corporation), so its ownership information is concealed. When providing owner anonymity, the corporation is an effective vehicle for doing so. However, it will primarily be determined by the jurisdiction in which the corporation is formed. In some jurisdictions, the incorporation process allows corporations' ownership information to remain anonymous or difficult to discover. Nominee directors and officers, for example, can be used to register a corporation in Wyoming and Nevada (C or S). This effectively keeps such corporations' true ownership information anonymous and private.

Ownership anonymity provides privacy and security while protecting the S Corporation and its shareholders from frivolous lawsuits. It can also be used to combat harassment and stalking.

Credibility and Acceptance of S Corporation

A corporation (S or C) is a common and well-known business structure that is widely accepted by the public and the business world. The corporation is a well-established, tried-and-true business structure. No other business structure outperforms the corporation regarding public credibility, familiarity, and acceptance. As a result, doing business as a corporation (S or C) can help to bridge the credibility and trust gap with the public quickly.

Transferability of S Corporation Shares

S Corporation shares can generally be transferred (sold or gifted). S Corporation stock can be freely transferred without a restricting or encumbering provision in the S-bylaws corporations or an existing buy-sell agreement.

If a buy-sell agreement exists, it will specify the terms and conditions under which an S Corporation shareholder may sell, buy, or otherwise transfer their S Corporation shares. Assume no existing buy-sell agreement or contrary provisions in the S-bylaws exist. In that case, the corporation's stock of the S Corporation may be freely bought, sold, or otherwise transferred.

However, suppose the transfer of the S-stock corporation results in a violation of the Internal Revenue Code's S Corporation rules (by the S Corporation). In that case, the S Corporation will lose its S-status automatically. For example, if an S-stock corporation is sold to a non-US resident alien (knowingly or unknowingly), the S-S-status corporation will be terminated. This is because non-US resident aliens are prohibited from owning stock in an S Corporation. The S Corporation will then be converted to a C Corporation (its former status).

WHAT IS THE PROCEDURE FOR TRANSFERRING S CORPORATION STOCK?

1. Assume there are relevant provisions in the S-bylaws of the corporation or a buy-sell agreement. In that case, the stock transfer procedures outlined in the relevant document must be strictly adhered to.

2. To memorialize the terms of the transfer, you will typically need to draft a stock-transfer agreement. The stock can be sold in exchange for money or gifted to another person for no monetary or other consideration.

3. The parties should then sign the stock-transfer agreement. If the transaction is a purchase, the seller will sign the stock certificate, and the buyer will pay the seller. If the stock transfer certificate is a gift, the owner simply signs it and gives it to the recipient.

4. The secretary of the board of directors should then record the stock transfer in the S-stock corporation's ledger.

5. Make and have the new stockholder sign a document agreeing to the corporation being taxed as an S Corporation. The contract must be both signed and notarized.

One of the requirements for receiving and maintaining S-status is that all S-shareholder corporations must consent (in signed writing) to the corporation being taxed as an S Corporation. The consent should then be recorded in the S Corporation's business records.

PROSPECTS FOR TAKING THE COMPANY PUBLIC IN THE FUTURE

C-corporation shares are preferred by public investors more than any other business structure. They specifically prefer Delaware C Corporations. Due to tax law and the structure of their governing documents, venture capitalists cannot invest in S Corporations.

Furthermore, because the S Corporation has a shareholder limit of 100, conducting a meaningful IPO in which the company's shares are supposed to be made available to hundreds of thousands, if not millions, of shareholders is nearly impossible. As a result, an S Corporation is unsuitable if you intend to seek significant external financing or to conduct your corporation's initial public offering (IPO).

However, it is possible to begin operating as an S Corporation and, whenever you want to prepare for external financing or an IPO, revoke your corporation's S-status and begin operating as a C Corporation.

REAL ESTATE INVESTING WITH AN S CORPORATION

The S Corporation offers no additional benefits to the average passive real estate investor. However, it may be useful to real estate operators whose primary business is real estate.

An S Corporation does not always assist in lowering self-employment tax.

Real estate investing is not commonly considered a viable business or trade. Profits from real estate investing are thus exempt from self-employment tax. They are only subject to income tax (perhaps net investment income tax).

This means that, in most cases, a typical real estate investor (i.e., a passive investor whose real estate activities do not constitute a trade or business) does not have to pay self-employment tax. This also implies that if a typical passive real estate investor used an S Corporation, the investor would not be merely reducing their self-employment tax liability.

CHAPTER 6

SHAREHOLDER DISTRIBUTIONS

A shareholder in an S Corporation is a complicated concept. The basis is important to understand because if an S Corporation incurs a loss, a shareholder cannot accept the loss if it exceeds the basis. Simply put, the basis is the value of your corporation's stock shares. Simply put, the basis is the amount of money invested in the corporation by the owner. Assume you set up an S Corporation and deposit $1,000 into the company's checking account before you start a business. Your initial investment is $1,000. You will almost certainly lend money to the company to keep it operating while doing business. Debt basis can be confusing when discussing the S Corporation basis; however, it is an essential concept for you to understand as a business owner.

According to the courts, a shareholder must meet two basic requirements to have an adjusted basis for a loan to an S Corporation. The first and most basic requirement is that the debt is owed directly by the S Corporation to the shareholder. If a shareholder simply guarantees the S-debt, Corporation's the shareholder does not have a basis in debt to the S Corporation. [14] The shareholder must also have an actual "economic outlay," according to the second requirement.

In addition to cash, you may have contributed property such as a computer, automobile, tools, or other items. The shareholder basis would rise due to capital contributions, ordinary income, investment income, and gains. Basis decreases include charitable contributions, Section 179 depreciation (accelerated depreciation), non-deductible expenses such as shareholder life insurance, one-half of meals and entertainment, tax penalties, net losses, and shareholder distributions. Basis adjustments are usually calculated at the end of a company's fiscal year.

These changes to the property's foundation must be made in a specific order. First, any income items such as ordinary income, dividend income, interest earned, passive income, and capital gains would be added to any basis. Distributions reduce the basis, followed by deduction, loss items, and current losses.

Consider stock basis the same way you would consider a bank account. Any deposits and the interest income the bank pays will be credited to your bank account. Inflows of cash, equipment, and profit would accompany stock basis deposits. A deduction from your bank account is money taken out for yourself, money used to pay bills, and fees you must pay. A decrease in stock basis would be any profit distributions you took for yourself and any expenses you paid on behalf of the corporation. Your basis, like a bank account, can never fall below zero. We can talk about reasonable compensation and distributions now that we know the basics.

A substantial amount of compensation to be packaged for an S Corporation shareholder is most likely one of the rifts in the Tax Code that has been abused. When explaining to a client why they should be taxed as an S Corporation, we would tell them that S Corporations are flow-through entities, which means that when profits flow over to the shareholder, they are not subject to self-employment tax. However, this is an incorrect statement that should be investigated immediately. S Corporation shareholders must be fairly compensated. As a result, a portion of their compensation is subject to FICA taxes, which are simply another name for self-employment tax. However, the theory guiding the introduction of the S-Election is that a shareholder can only choose what they pay self-employment tax on because it is only paid through FICA taxes and reasonable compensation. What constitutes fair compensation, then?

According to Internal Revenue Service policy, distributions from S Corporations can be classified as compensation and subject to FICA taxes. This policy, supported by several Revenue Procedures (Rev. Proc.) on the subject, is comprehensive in scope, and the Courts were left to decide how to interpret the Service's stance.

Following an audit, the IRS determined that all payments to the shareholder were compensation and assessed FICA taxes on the amount taken. In this case, the company agreed that the sole shareholder would be an employee. During a recession, the shareholder moved personal funds from their bank account to the company's bank account. Glass Blocks complained that the payments made to the sole shareholder were simply loan repayments. The IRS responded to their claim by claiming that the funds transferred were capital contributions and that the distributions received by the shareholder were compensation. The United States Tax Court requested evidence to prove that the funds transferred were loans made by the taxpayer. The court later determined that four factors contradicted the company's claim that the funds were loans.

The court determined that there was no promissory note or written agreement between the shareholder and the company regarding a loan from the shareholder; no interest was charged to the company on the repayment; no security was provided for the loan, and there was no amortization schedule of fixed repayments for the loan.

The company would have a dividend payment policy if the shareholder-owned stock in any corporation with earnings. Most public companies, for example, report quarterly earnings. Dividends are usually paid quarterly if they pay them.

As practitioners, we are unlikely to deal with publicly traded companies, but a distribution policy must be in place. Profit distributions in the policy can be specified to be paid monthly, quarterly, or yearly. Because no other corporation pays dividends in this manner, a shareholder cannot receive distributions at arbitrary intervals such as weekly or biweekly. In addition, the IRS could rule that a weekly or biweekly distribution payment is a disguised salary. As a result, they are required to pay FICA taxes.

To summarize, determining fair compensation for an S-shareholder corporation is difficult. However, we have discovered some guidelines that we can follow. For example, it's clear from the examples above that fair compensation doesn't just happen; it varies by company. A client's condition does not always apply to another. Unfortunately for them, there are no simple solutions for determining what is reasonable compensation. Simply put, we must approach each business differently. Owners of S Corporations who perform services for the corporation must be fairly compensated for their efforts.

CHAPTER 7

TAXES AND HOW TO FILL THEM

The S Corporation has made a special election with the IRS and is now taxed as an LLC or partnership. As a result, an S Corporation is not subject to corporate income tax, and its earnings are taxed "pass-through," which means that the company's profits or losses are passed through to the shareholders or owners. As a result, S Corporation's earnings are not taxed twice.

An S Corporation protects its owners from liability while avoiding federal income taxation. It is a type of corporation found in IRC Subchapter S of Chapter 1.

The first step in forming an S Corporation is to incorporate it as a regular corporation. To do so, you must file and submit certain documents, such as a certificate of incorporation and articles of incorporation, with the SEC or another government agency. You will also be required to pay the fees of the institutions.

To obtain the S Corporation designation, you and all other stockholders must sign Form 2553 after successfully incorporating your company. Income taxes will be filed and paid individually by you and all other owners on your returns following the successful tax identification of your business as an S Corporation.

To qualify, your corporation must meet the following requirements, according to the Internal Revenue Service:

- It must be based or domiciled in the United States.
- It must have only allowable stockholders, including individuals, estates, and specific types of trusts. It must exclude non-resident alien stockholders and business entities such as partnerships and corporations.
- It must have only allowable stockholders.
- The total number of stockholders cannot exceed 100.
- The company must have only one stock classification.
- It cannot be a disqualified corporation under the S Corp structure, such as certain types of financial institutions, domestic and international sales corporations, or insurance companies.

HOW ARE S CORPORATION SHAREHOLDERS TAXED?

The shareholders report their income/losses on individual tax returns and pay any required income tax at their tax rates. An S Corporation with two or more shareholders is taxed similarly to a partnership. In contrast, an S Corporation with one shareholder is taxed similarly to a sole proprietorship. An S Corporation does not pay federal income tax at the corporate level.

1120S IRS Form

IRS Form 1120S is completed and filed by an S corporation (US Corporation Income Tax Return for an S Corporation). Form 1120S is merely an informational return in which the S Corporation discloses its income and losses for the tax year, as well as the allocable share of the income and losses for each of its shareholders.

K-1 Schedule

In addition to filing Form 1120S, the S Corporation sends a Schedule K-1 (Shareholder's Share of Income, Credits, and Deductions) to each shareholder.

TAX CONSEQUENCES OF ALLOCATED VS. DISTRIBUTED SHARES

The Schedule K-1 for each shareholder contains specific information about the shareholder's allocable share of the S-income corporation and deductions. Each shareholder must then report these figures on their tax return (IRS Form 1040) and pay tax on their share of the S-income corporation regardless of whether the income was distributed to the shareholder.

Profits and losses of the S Corporation are allocated based on the percentage of ownership interest in the S Corporation and retained earnings.

Although an S Corporation can keep its profits as retained earnings, those earnings are taxed. On the other hand, retained earnings of a C-corporation are not taxed until they are distributed as dividends, salaries, or bonuses.

When an S Corporation makes a profit during the tax year, it does not have to pay corporate income tax on that profit. Instead, it can pay out some of its profits as dividends to shareholders, reinvest some of its profits as retained earnings, or do both.

Because the S Corporation is a pass-through entity, its profits are passed through to its shareholders, and all of the S-net corporation's profits are taxable to the S-shareholders. In other words, whether the S Corporation distributes profits to shareholders as dividends, keeps profits for itself as retained earnings, or does a little of both, S Corporation shareholders pay tax on the S-net corporation's profit. But take note of two things:

If the S Corporation distributes profits to its shareholders (as dividends), they do not have to pay tax on that distribution. However, if the company retains the profits, the shareholders must still pay income taxes on all of the S-profits Corporation (which includes the retained earnings).

In other words, the S-shareholders corporation pays income tax on money (retained earnings) that they never received (and will never receive directly) because retained earnings are money retained by the S Corporation to be used for future reasonable business activities.

| HOW TO AVOID DOUBLE TAXATION

To avoid being taxed twice on the same income, it is critical to understand what the IRS says about an S Corporation regarding federal income taxation.

Many investors consider this to be one of the property's most desirable features because a regular corporation's taxable income is subject to double taxation. The first occurs at the corporate level, while the second occurs at the individual level in the form of stockholder dividend income taxes.

In the earlier chapter on LLCs, you saw how double taxation on a regular corporation looks. The pass-through income taxation scheme eliminates double taxation if you choose to incorporate as an S Corporation. Because its profits and losses are reported on the individual tax returns of its shareholders, an S Corp is exempt from paying income taxes.

This benefit, however, is not available to all S Corps. Some states and municipalities have enacted legislation that denies such advantages to these businesses.

Take, for example, the city of New York. The city imposes an 8.85% corporate income tax on S Corporations. However, if the corporation can show that it operates outside New York, its income will be exempt from this flat rate. Similarly, California imposes a franchise tax of 1.5% of an S Corporation's annual net income or $800, whichever is greater.

Form 1120S will be used to file your income tax return if you choose an S Corporation; Profits, losses, and deductions of shareholders are itemized on Schedule K-1, just like they are for LLCs.

For tax purposes, the IRS regards an S Corp as a simple pass-through entity. This means that taxes on its income are eventually passed down to its owners for them to pay income taxes. Except for that, this business entity operates similarly to regular corporations.

Many states use federal data on taxpayers' total income to calculate state taxes. As a result, it is critical to file and pay federal income taxes correctly.

You pay income taxes as an S Corporation owner based on your distributive share of the company's net income. If you have a single LLC and have elected to be one, you own the entire net income. These taxes will be reported on Form 1040.

Double taxation is one of the most common complaints about a regular corporation. While the law prohibits double taxation on individuals, double taxation on regular corporation income applies to two different parties. An S Corporation does not have this problem. Because it is only a pass-through entity for tax purposes, its income is taxed as the owners' income. Unlike regular corporations, which are taxed at corporate and personal income levels due to dividends, S Corp income is taxed only once.

TAXES ON SELF-EMPLOYMENT

Dividends are paid to shareholders of a regular corporation in exchange for their investment. However, S Corp owners must pay regular income taxes on their share of the company's earnings, but the IRS does not consider them self-employed. As a result, you will not have to pay self-employment taxes on your portion of the company's income. However, if you work for the company and receive a salary, you must pay FICA or self-employment taxes such as Social Security and Medicare. As a result, S Corp owner-employees are subject to this tax.

OTHER S CORPORATION TAXES

Your S Corporation will have to pay other business taxes like any other business. These are employment or payroll taxes, state-imposed excise and sales taxes, and state-specific taxes on S Corps such as gross receipts, franchise, and income taxes.

HOW MUCH CAN SMALL BUSINESSES EARN BEFORE TAXES?

According to the IRS, all businesses, except partnerships, must file an annual income tax return. Partnerships must file an information return. You must pay employment taxes if you have employees.

Business owners who earn less than $400 in profits are exempt from the self-employment tax, which is the only tax you can avoid. The IRS is unlikely to audit your small business until it starts making money. Even if you are losing money, filing your taxes is essential to avoid legal problems and take advantage of deductions.

WHEN SHOULD YOU PAY SMALL BUSINESS TAXES?

As important as the types of taxes you must pay, you must also consider when you must pay them. Many business owners pay their taxes only once before the IRS's deadline. However, many business owners must regularly pay estimated self-employment and income taxes.

The estimated tax is the tax you pay throughout the year based on your estimated taxable income. According to the IRS, business owners, including sole proprietors, stockholders, and partners, should make quarterly estimated tax payments if they believe they will owe $1000 or more in taxes when their federal or state tax returns are filed.

Form 1040-ES can be used to calculate your estimated taxes. You can also use your previous year's income, tax deductions, and credits as a starting point. Another helpful resource is last year's federal tax return. When filing your tax return, you can deduct the estimated tax payments you made throughout the year from your total liability. The federal income tax is a "pay-as-you-go" tax, which means that if you don't make the required payments when they're due, you'll have to pay interest and penalties.

After you figure out the number and e-file the tax form, you have several options for paying the IRS: IRS Pay By Card, which allows you to pay with a debit or credit card online, or IRS Direct Pay, which allows the IRS to deduct the money you owe from your checking (or savings) account. You can also pay the IRS over the phone.

The quarterly estimated tax payments for every respective quarter are due every April 15th, June 15th, Sept 15th, and Jan 15th of the following year.

Quarterly Estimated Tax Due Date

Period You Get Paid	Tax Due Date
January 1– March 31	April 15
April 1– May 31	June 15
June 1– August 31	September 15
September 1– December 31	January 15 of the following year

In contrast to salaried employees, whose employers withhold a certain amount of tax from each paycheck, freelancers, sole proprietors, and business owners bear the entire tax burden.

Furthermore, individuals who are partners in corporations are frequently required to pay quarterly taxes if they estimate they owe at least $500 in taxes.

On the other hand, business owners who fail to submit at least 90% of their owed taxes face severe penalties. As a result, working with a tax professional who can double-check the amount owed is recommended.

HOW TAX DEDUCTIONS AND CREDITS AFFECT YOUR BUSINESS TAX RATE

As previously stated, with the 20% deduction available to sole proprietors and other pass-through entities, determining your business's final tax rate is more complicated than simply multiplying net income by your tax rate. The following is a brief overview of three factors that influence your final tax bill (and we will discuss them in detail in later sections).

- **Operating Losses (Net):** Some businesses may have a net operating loss deduction carried forward from the previous year to reduce the amount of taxable income in the current year.

- **Deductions for taxes:** Many business owners want to take advantage of tax breaks to reduce their taxable income. Yes, some deductions can have a significant impact on your bottom line. For example, the Section 179 deduction allows businesses to deduct the total cost of an asset, such as machinery or a vehicle, in the year of purchase.
- **Tax Credits:** Many businesses qualify for tax credits, reducing the tax amount they must pay. In some ways, tax credits are superior to tax deductions because they allow you to deduct the amount of tax owed on a dollar-for-dollar basis. For example, a company that uses alternative energy or fuel may be eligible for the tax credit.

Because of the tax breaks and credits, two businesses with the same net income from the previous year can pay different federal income taxes.

ON AVERAGE, HOW MUCH TAX DO SMALL BUSINESSES PAY?

According to Small Business Administration data, small businesses of all types pay an average tax rate of about 19.8%. Small businesses with one owner pay an average tax rate of 13.3%, while those with more than one owner pay an average tax rate of 23.6%. Small S corporations pay an average tax rate of 26.9%.

Because they have earned more money, some corporations have higher tax rates. That makes sense when you consider that 18% of small S corporations earn $100,000 or more in net income, but nearly 60% of small businesses with one owner earn less than $10,000.

HOW TO HANDLE BUSINESS TAXES

You now understand what your company can expect from the tax, and you may be wondering how to prepare so that you are not caught off guard when it comes time to pay your taxes. Because no two businesses pay the same amount of tax, each approach will be slightly different.

Any business owner can do the best for their company to save money ahead of time. Set aside 30-40% of your quarterly income to cover federal and state taxes, preferably at the rate applicable to your small business. It is especially important when you have just started your business and do not yet understand your company's tax liabilities.

As you save your tax refund:

1. Are you new to the world of small business? Set aside at least 30% of your pay every time you get paid.
2. Have you recently made a profit? Then save your 30% monthly.
3. Is your profit reasonably consistent year after year? Consider dividing your net income from last year by four. Take 30% of that figure and try to save that much every quarter.

Another good practice is to keep tax money separate in a business bank. This way, you won't squander money that could have gone to the IRS. You can also set up automatic transfers from your business bank account to another separate account (quarterly or monthly) to ensure that you save enough money to cover your tax bill.

You shouldn't be concerned about underpaying or miscalculating the amount owed. According to the IRS, if you pay the same amount in taxes each quarter as you did the previous year, you are protected by the "safe harbor rule," which states that you will not be penalized for underpayment.

For more about this rule, you can read on the **IRS website** (https://www.irs.gov/taxtopics/tc306)

| CHAPTER 8 |

S CORPORATION MISTAKES AND HOW TO AVOID THEM

| EXCESSIVE OVERHEAD

O verhead can quickly become unmanageable, especially given the limited number of requirements for effective freight broker agents. Computers, phones, and occasional travel are required, but they can be used in any room, from a living room to a small, basic office.

While modern technologies are beneficial, costs and budgetary constraints must be considered. Self-employed agents must exercise caution regarding expenses such as software, bookkeeping, and time-consuming administrative tasks.

FAILURE TO EVOLVE

A wide range of additional skills is required to run a successful business. Agents who want to grow their business often find it difficult because hiring full-time employees for back-office assistance and other tasks is such a risk.

Even in an increasingly high-tech environment, S Corporation issues can be addressed by employing tried-and-true low-tech techniques such as well-targeted phone follow-ups and lightning-fast customer service.

COMPLACENCY

For a regular business, there is a lot of competition. The thing to avoid is looking for new ways to improve it. Someone will always be able to do things differently and possibly better. A successful businessperson is always looking for ways to improve.

NOT EMBRACING TECHNOLOGY

You may have heard of this thing called the Internet. Intelligent companies, including freight brokers, have fully embraced technology. Technology can assist you in shortening processes and automating routine tasks. As a result, you will have more time to devote to your business's marketing and other revenue-generating aspects.

In contrast, installing processes entails defining clear workflows so that your employees fully understand what is expected of them in a situation. Many business owners believe that their employees are equally capable of dealing with volatile situations. This, however, is not always the case. You may have had to learn how to do things from the ground up; expecting your employees to do the same is a waste of time.

Instead, use technology to automate the most unimportant tasks and create good documentation that instructs your employees on what to do in various situations. They can then improve those processes by building on them. Returning to technology, successful freight brokers make use of a variety of software programs.

To handle bookkeeping and accounting, you'll need software. This is a must-have for all businesses. Don't mistake saving paper receipts and manually entering them into a spreadsheet. Invest in high-quality software, and you will undoubtedly reap the benefits in the long run.

| INADEQUATE FUNDING

Always ensure that you have enough cash in the bank and are adequately capitalized. If you aren't, you're on your way to a life of agony in which every business decision feels like pulling teeth. In your personal life, imagine having to choose between food and water because you only have enough money for one expense.

That may appear absurd, but many business owners put themselves and their companies in this position by being naive. Fortunately, you are not naive because you are reading this book and educating yourself. On the other hand, undercapitalization puts even the most promising businesses out of work.

When starting a business, most owners try to save as much money as possible. This is understandable given the low cash flow and high costs. However, there is a distinction between cutting costs and shooting yourself in the foot. You should bootstrap your operations to the greatest extent possible, but not so far that you can't afford to buy the tools you need to succeed.

The profit equation has two components: costs and revenues. Many businesses concentrate solely on costs, believing revenues will care for themselves. To generate revenue, however, you must actively invest money. Take note that I said "invest" rather than "spend." Purchasing software is an investment that will pay for itself many times over in utility.

Similarly, hiring and paying great employees who will generate revenue for you is an investment rather than an expense. As a business owner, your primary goal is to allocate capital. Your employees will be able to manage the day-to-day operations of the company.

However, they will only be able to do so efficiently if you provide them with the necessary resources to do a good job. If you don't do this, it's akin to purchasing a high-end sports car, refusing to fill the tank with premium fuel, or avoiding long-lasting purchasing tires.

INEFFECTIVE PROCEDURES AND PROCESSES

A process distinguishes a one-person operation from a large corporation. When you hire even one person, you are responsible for assisting them in carrying out their responsibilities effectively. They must perform well and earn more than you do.

No technology allows people to transfer their thoughts to another person directly, and your employee is unlikely to be a mind reader. The only thing you can do to help them is to create as many standardized processes as possible and procedures that can be repeated repeatedly.

As a business owner, you will spend most of your time refining and tuning your processes to ensure everything runs smoothly. You'll spend your entire day putting out fires if you don't. So, focus on developing highly repeatable processes that even inexperienced employees can understand; don't leave loose ends, and document everything. This is what will assist you in growing your business.

NARROW BUSINESS BOOK

This error occurs because these business owners do not consider marketing a continuous activity as important as operations. There will be no operations if there is no marketing. Marketing is more important than operations regarding freight brokerage because your customers are always looking for brokers who can offer them lower rates.

Your competitors will always try to entice your customers away from you. While providing excellent service is a perfect way to keep them on board with you, it does not protect you from the customer's business failing. You must constantly advertise yourself and implement strong marketing processes to keep your company at the forefront of every customer's mind.

You'll have a complete marketing strategy ready when you're finished. Understand, however, that even the best marketing plans require your commitment and desire. You will struggle if you're unwilling to invest the same energy in marketing as you do in your operations.

DEAD INVOICES

Dead invoices are a common issue in the freight brokerage industry. Your customers typically pay you after 60 days, whereas your suppliers expect payment within 30 days. This results in a cash-flow gap. You can easily overcome this obstacle if your book of business is strong. However, new businesses rarely have large customer bases that they can rely on.

Most customers will treat you according to your expectations. If you do not communicate your terms and payment process, they will most likely take advantage of you and delay payment. When you combine this situation with a limited business book, you have a recipe for disaster.

It is your processes that will save you. It makes sense to automate invoice tracking and collection as much as possible. Automation is expensive, but you're less likely to miss payments due to poor cash reconciliation to invoices or lose a customer dispute because you couldn't pull up a record in time. It all comes down to how much money you're willing to put up. Most business owners do not consider invoice and payment collection worthwhile investment areas, assuming it will happen automatically once the job is completed.

You must, however, constantly negotiate credit cycles and work to maximize cash flow. Allowing your invoices to collect dust is a sure way never to get paid. The key is to develop processes that allow you to efficiently collect payments and follow up with your customers on time. Dispute resolution should be accompanied by processes allowing your employees to track and resolve disputes quickly.

FOCUSING SOLELY ON THE MONEY

Because you're in business to make money, it's natural that you'll be concerned about the financial aspects of each load that comes your way. Many newcomers enter these transactions without considering the consequences of their actions. There is no such thing as a free lunch in this industry, and there is always a catch with such loads.

Prioritize relationships while keeping monetary terms fair to all parties. You may have to give up a few margin points here and there, but that doesn't mean you have to cripple yourself to succeed in this business. Everyone you deal with will try to drive a hard bargain, but that's normal. Everyone benefits from the best deals. That is what keeps people returning to you. So, concentrate on the value you can offer people, and you'll have no trouble making money.

| CHAPTER 9 |

DEDUCTION TACTICS

The tax deduction, also known as the "tax write-off," is an expense that can be deducted from your taxable income. You take your business expenses and deduct them from your income. It only allows you to pay a lower tax bill, and the deducted expenses must meet IRS tax deduction criteria.

| HOW TO CLAIM BUSINESS STARTUP TAX BREAKS

Even if you can deduct some of your business's startup costs, there are some limitations. Business expenses are limited to $5,000 in deductions during the first year of operation. As a result, if your startup costs more than $50,000, your first-year tax deduction will be reduced by more than $50,000.

For example, if your startup costs $52,000, your first-year deductions will be reduced by $2,000, bringing the total to $3,000. You will lose the entire deduction if your expenses exceed $55,000. The remaining costs can then be amortized and deducted over 15 years, beginning with the second operation year.

HOW TO CLAIM BUSINESS STARTUP DEDUCTIONS ON TAX RETURNS

You must report the first-year deduction on your business tax form if you take it. Schedule C is for sole proprietors, Form 1120 is for corporations, and K-1 is for a partnership or S corporation. The amortized deductions can be claimed on Form 4562 in subsequent years (Depreciation and Amortization).

The deduction is then carried over to your Schedule C under other business expenses if you are a sole proprietor or to the corporate or partnership income tax form if you are a corporation or partnership. You can then continue to claim it for the remainder of the amortization period.

TOP SMALL BUSINESS TAX BREAKS

The following are the most common business expenses that can be deducted. Keep this checklist in mind when attempting to deduct business taxes. Please remember that some of the deductions may not apply to your business. Consult your CPA or tax advisor before claiming them.

Promotion and Advertising

Advertising and promotion costs are entirely deductible. The cost of printing business brochures and cards; hiring someone to design your business logo; purchasing ad space in online media or print; launching a new website; sending cards to clients; sponsoring an event; and running a social media marketing campaign are all included in this category.

However, money paid to sponsor political events or campaigns, or to influence legislation, cannot be deducted (such as lobbying)

Commercial Insurance

You can deduct the premiums paid for business insurance, which may include:

- Liability coverage.
- Property coverage for your furniture, buildings, and equipment.
- Group health, vision, and dental insurance for your employees.
- Workers' compensation coverage.
- Malpractice insurance or professional liability.
- Auto insurance for your business vehicle.
- Business interruption insurance covers losses if your business is forced to close due to a fire or other unforeseen event.

Business Meals

Generally, you can deduct half of the qualifying costs for food and beverages. To be eligible for this deduction, you must:

- The meals cannot be extravagant under the circumstances; the expenses must be a necessary and ordinary part of doing business, and the employee or business owners must be present at the meals.
- You can also deduct 50% of your employees' meals, such as buying burgers for dinner if your team works late. Meals provided at office picnics and parties are also fully deductible.
- Maintain documentation demonstrating the date and location of the meal, the amount of each expense, and the business relationship of the individual with whom you dined. Write the purpose of the meal and any other relevant information on the back of the receipt.

Commercial Use of Your Vehicle

Do you use your vehicle for business purposes? You can deduct the entire operating cost if you only use your vehicle for business purposes. You can only deduct business-related expenses when you use them for personal and business trips.

Bank Charges

Having separate credit cards and bank accounts for your business is always a good idea. Monthly or annual service fees, overdraft fees, and transfer fees assessed by your credit card or bank are tax deductible. Transactions or merchant fees paid to a third-party payment processor can also be deducted (i.e., Stripe or PayPal). On the other hand, fees for personal credit or bank accounts are not deductible.

Contract Labor

You can deduct their fees as business expenses if you hire independent contractors or freelancers to help you with your business. If you pay a contractor more than $600 during the tax year, you must send them a Form 1099-NEC by January 31st.

Education Expenses

Education expenses are fully deductible because they increase your expertise and add value to your business. To determine whether your workshop or class qualifies, the IRS considers whether the expenses maintain or improve the skills required in your current business.

Depreciation

Suppose you purchased equipment, furniture, or other business assets. In that case, depreciation rules require you to spread the expenses of those assets over the years you will use them rather than deducting the entire amount in a single hit.

Rental Cost

You can deduct the rental payments if you rent business equipment or a location for your business. Even if you have a home office, remember that rent paid on your home cannot be deducted as a business expense. However, the rent can be deducted from the home office expense. For more information, please see the following item.

| PERSONAL TAX BREAKS FOR BUSINESS OWNERS

Aside from the deductions mentioned above, you can claim on Form 1065 for Schedule C, and there are a couple of tax breaks that small business owners commonly claim on their tax returns.

Health-Care Costs

Aside from insurance premiums, some out-of-pocket medical expenses are deductible and itemized on Schedule A, such as office copays and prescription drug costs.

On Schedule 1 of Form 1040, self-employed business owners can deduct health insurance premiums for themselves and dependents (such as their spouse). You cannot, however, deduct health care premiums if you can participate in a plan through your spouse's employer.

Donations to Charities

Charitable contributions cannot be deducted as business expenses by LLCs, sole proprietorships, or partners. The deductions, however, may be claimed on the business owners' tax returns. Donations must be made to qualified organizations to qualify.

Cash contributions can be claimed as "above-the-line" deductions on Form 1040. If you want to deduct more than the limit (in 2020, taxpayers could claim up to $300), you can itemize your deductions on Schedule A, which is attached to Form 1040.

Contributions to Retirement Plans

Employee retirement contributions can also be deducted as a business expense. If you only contribute to your retirement accounts, you can claim the contribution on Schedule 1 and attach it to Form 1040. Your plan type determines the amount you can deduct. Following the IRS's instructions, you can calculate your retirement plan contribution and deduction.

Expenses for Child and Dependent Care

If you pay someone to care for your child or another dependent while working, you may be eligible for the child and dependent care credit. To be eligible, the person receiving care must be a 13-year-old child, your spouse, or any other dependents who are mentally or physically incapable of self-care.

The credit will be worth approximately 20-35% of your allowable expenses based on your income. In addition, allowable costs are limited to $3,000 for one dependent and $6,000 for more than two dependents. IRS Publication 503 contains more information on the child and dependent care credit. Remember to include Form 2441 with your Form 1040 to claim it.

THE COMPLETE TAX DEDUCTION

So, what exactly is a 100% tax deduction? It is a business expense that can be completely deducted from your taxable income taxes. For small businesses, the following expenses are completely deductible:

- Office supplies, such as printers, scanners, and computers; Furniture purchased solely for office use in the year of purchase.
- Employee and client gifts, up to $25 per person per year.
- Business travel and related expenses, such as hotels and car rentals.
- Yearly business phone bills.
- If you are self-employed, pay your health insurance premiums, which are fully deductible.

HOW TO CLAIM TAX BREAKS AS A BUSINESS OWNER

You must complete a Schedule C tax form to claim small-business tax deductions as a sole proprietorship. The taxable income for the year is calculated using Form Schedule C. Report this profit and calculate the taxes owed on your personal 1040 form.

Understandably, no one wants to pay taxes or the tax filing fee. Tax deductions are an important tool for lowering the amount of tax owed. Even if the IRS comes knocking, keeping good records will help you get those deductions. If you have any questions about your business tax return, always seek the advice of a tax professional.

CONCLUSION

Thank you for taking the time to read this book. A small business may benefit significantly from being an S Corp. This is due to its ability to issue a wide range of stocks with virtually no restrictions on who can own shares and a virtually unlimited number of shareholders. An S Corporation's profits are not taxed. However, filing a tax return with the IRS using Form 1120S is required, as is providing Form K-1 to all members to report income when filing individual tax returns.

One critical requirement is that an S Corporation pays its shareholders who work for the company a reasonable salary. If the company did not pay its employees' salaries at fair market value, the IRS might reclassify the shareholder's distribution as "wages."

Because states treat S Corporations similarly to the IRS, most states do not tax their profits. However, some states tax S Corporations at the corporate and shareholder levels.

S corporations are notoriously difficult for business owners to grasp (and the pass-through concept overall). It can be perplexing to pay personal income tax on a corporation's profits when the owner does not receive them in cash. The inverse relationship between the owner's wages and the corporation's taxable profits can also be perplexing. On the other hand, the FICA tax savings are difficult to beat and are the primary reason for S corporations' popularity.

Good luck!

QUICKBOOKS ONLINE FOR BEGINNERS 2024

The Most Updated Guide to QuickBooks

for Small Business Owners

THOMAS NEWTON

INTRODUCTION

QuickBooks is an accounting program that helps you manage your company's finances. Despite its small size, it has significantly impacted the accounting software industry with its handy evolution over the years, including QuickBooks' new features and functionality to accommodate small businesses. QuickBooks is the ideal application for managing your financial activities when starting a small business.

You can easily start and run a small business without dealing with additional accounting issues. When combined with monitoring client information, sales, and transactions, it becomes a complete solution for small and medium-sized businesses.

With this book tutorial, you'll be able to set up your QuickBooks online in no time by entering your company's information into the dashboard and creating entries for vendors, customers, and payroll. You will also learn how to create customer-facing financial reports and how to file your taxes on time with the help of this book. You will be able to keep track of the progress of your company's operations and financial performance by using this.

| CHAPTER 1 |

ALL ABOUT QUICKBOOKS ONLINE

| HOW DOES QUICKBOOKS WORK?

QuickBooks is the widely used software for business accounting software for managing revenue and spending and keeping track of financial health. Customers can be invoiced, invoices can be paid, reports can be generated, and taxes can be prepared. QuickBooks offers a variety of solutions to meet various company needs, including QuickBooks Online, QuickBooks Desktop, QuickBooks Payroll, and QuickBooks Time.

While there are several alternatives available, you are not required to sign up for all QuickBooks services at once. You may begin with a single program, such as accounting or payroll software, and add others as your business grows. If you outgrow a service, you may select whether to eliminate or upgrade it.

A typical QuickBooks setup would look like this: you sign up for the accounting software, then install QuickBooks Live to personalize your setup completely. As your company expands, you add full-time workers, contractors, and freelancers. After that, you may sign up for QuickBooks Payroll to automate monthly payments and QuickBooks Time to monitor billable hours.

BENEFITS OF QUICKBOOKS ONLINE

1. QuickBooks Online is a popular choice for accountants and small business owners because it can be accessed anywhere and on almost any device. You will need an internet connection because the software and your data are saved on Intuit servers in the cloud.
2. QuickBooks Online can also be set up to generate invoices for billable time and expenses for each transaction and provide quick email reports that go along with the transactions.
3. QuickBooks Online Plus is required for inventory monitoring. Nonetheless, some inventory bells and whistles found in the desktop software are missing in the Plus version. If QuickBooks Online's inventory capabilities do not meet your needs, another option is to subscribe to a third-party inventory program.
4. Progress invoices are features available in QuickBooks Online Plus and allow you to track task expenditures and profitability. On the other hand, sales orders are not supported by QuickBooks Online.
5. Intuit releases new QuickBooks Online features and enhancements every month. As a result, the boundaries between online and offline are blurring. Try QuickBooks Online for free for 30 days to see if the software meets your requirements.

However, based on the advantages listed, QuickBooks online is unquestionably the best option. The confusion now revolves around selecting the best versions for accounting activities that meet your bookkeeping requirements and budget.

VERSIONS OF QUICKBOOKS

There are several factors to consider when developing an effective bookkeeping system:

1. While on the QuickBooks page, select "Plans & Pricing." QuickBooks Online provides several options.
2. Small businesses can use Simple Start, Plus, or Advanced, whereas independent contractors can use Self-Employed.

QuickBooks Online Self-Employed

This is the version with the fewest features. Users can access basic reports as well as income and expense tracking. These features include processing and printing checks, extremely simple invoicing, and a few designed reports to streamline bookkeeping processes. On the other hand, this version restricts data access to a single user at a time.

QuickBooks Online Plus

QuickBooks Online Plus has quickly become the most popular option with over a million users. Up to five people can use the system simultaneously and have complete control over their data while allowing for full bill management and payment, time tracking, and inventory tracking.

QuickBooks Online Advanced

QuickBooks Online's Advanced edition includes batch invoices and spending, company analytics, and premium care, but it costs more per month than the Plus edition. If you're unsure, QuickBooks Plus is your best bet. If you require complex accounting knowledge, you could upgrade to Online Advanced.

CHAPTER 2

GETTING STARTED

HOW TO GET STARTED WITH QUICKBOOKS ONLINE

Q uickBooks' interface, particularly the home screen, is genuinely user-friendly. QuickBooks Plus is the entry-level edition for small businesses, including essential features. QuickBooks is available on a variety of platforms.

In the address bar of your preferred browser, such as Chrome or Mozilla Firefox, type https://quickbooks.intuit.com/au/. If you have never used QuickBooks before, you must first create an account.

Sign in with your user ID, password, and other relevant information by clicking the button in the upper right corner of the screen and selecting QuickBooks Online.

After you sign in, you will have access to various features. A quick note: QuickBooks Online provides security alert notifications, which provide a warning when a transaction exceeds the limits set by the company's manager.

The homepage is displayed after successfully signing in. On one side of the page, there are some interesting features about the company, such as activities, sales, and purchase journal entries. Another section contains the Open Item report, a table displaying information about customer name, vendor name, account description, and amount.

The "New" button in the top right corner of the screen allows quick access to creating new transactions and other records. In contrast, the Search feature, built into this cloud app, allows users to find specific transactions by entering values of their choice.

Advanced Search: This provides more detailed options for finding a product/service, such as customer name, vendor name, transaction type, and more.

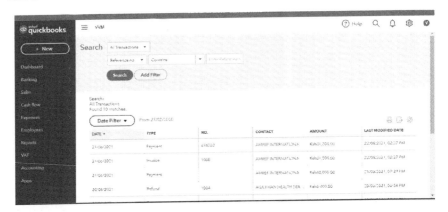

Recent Transactions: This feature allows the user to search for transactions by date and the amount that occurred within a specific time frame.

Show Less: This displays a list of all transactions sorted by date, as well as quick access options for updating and marking highlighted transactions as hidden or visible.

You can collapse the window by clicking the hamburger icon, which reveals options for canceling or completing a transaction, as well as access to the full-screen menu.

HOW TO ADD CUSTOMERS

Client names will appear on invoices and other forms created with this option. The itemized receipt in the section below in QuickBooks automatically reflects what you type here.

1. At the top, click on the *Customers* menu.
2. From the dropdown menu, choose *Customer Center*.
3. Choose *New Customer* in the dropdown menu and fill in the required details.
4. Click *Okay* to save the changes.

HOW TO ADD ITEMS

Items include anything your organization buys, sells, or resells, such as merchandise, shipping and handling costs, discounts, and sales tax (if applicable). They appear as a line on invoices or other sales documents. To add an item to your Item list, do the following:

1. Choose the command *Lists Item*. QuickBooks' item list window will appear.
2. To access the item menu, click the *Item* button in the lower-left corner of the item list window.
3. Press the *New* button. When you press this, QuickBooks will open the *New Item* box.
4. Using the boxes in the *New Item* window, describe the item you want to add. The first step is to decide what kind of item you want to include. QuickBooks includes additional description boxes.
5. After you've finished filling out the fields in the *New Item* window, click *Okay*. QuickBooks adds the item to the item list immediately after you describe it.

HOW TO MANAGE USERS

If a small business grows, it may add more QuickBooks users. The standard user and business admin retain complete and unrestricted access to QuickBooks. In contrast, users who become designated as reporting or time tracking, have limited access to certain QuickBooks files and functionalities. This means that if you add more users to your QuickBooks business, you'll need to create separate sub-company files and assign edit rights to each of the users to administer rights based on their needs and responsibilities.

To manage a user's role or permissions, do the following:

1. Sign into QuickBooks with a user profile that can manage users.
2. Select *Settings* at the gear button.
3. Select *Manage Users*.
4. Choose the user to be edited.
5. In the *User Type* dropdown menu, select the *New User* type. This section has four types of users: standard, company type, time tracking, and reporting.
6. Select the *User Settings*.
7. Select *Save*.

HOW TO ADD A SERVICE

To create an accurate record of your activity, transactions should include all information and services. The fields for items and services that can be imported are listed below. A more detailed overview of the fields can be found by manually inserting product and service items.

Before beginning a transaction, a chart of accounts must be created with the product/service name, price/rate, income account, and quantity as-of-date. The steps for adding a service in QuickBooks are as follows:

1. Click on *Products and Services* to access the product and services list in the left menu bar.
2. Click on the *New* button in the upper right corner of the screen.
3. Select whether the item you are adding is inventory, a non-inventory product, a service, or a bundle of products or services.
4. Complete the information requested for the item type you are adding. Click *Save* and close.

HOW TO USE PROJECTS

To track the profitability of your project, use projects in QuickBooks Online. From a single dashboard, you can enter project income, spending, and labor costs and run project-specific reports. You may even add existing transactions to new or current projects if necessary.

Projects is only accessible in QuickBooks Online Plus, Advanced, and Accountant.

To access this new function, follow the steps below to enable it in your QuickBooks account.

Turning on projects for current clients in QuickBooks Online Plus:

1. Click Gear, then Accounts and Settings
2. Now click on Advanced
3. Turn on projects

To create a new project, go through the following steps:

1. Go to Business overview and click Projects.
2. Choose New Project.
3. Enter the project name in the Project Name area.
4. Select the project's customer from the Customer dropdown menu.
5. Add any project-related notes or details to Notes.
6. Click Save.

After creating a project, both new and existing transactions can be added to it.

HOW TO CHECK YOUR COMPANY ID

This ID is used to access QuickBooks. It enables you to easily access your business, restore data, and perform other accounting tasks online. This could be an issue if you have many company files or QuickBooks accounts. A solid ID will assist you in finding a file among a terabyte of data.

The steps to check your ID in QuickBooks are as follows:

1. Navigate to the *Account and Settings* tab by clicking the setting icon.
2. Click on the *Billing & Subscriptions* section. The business ID is shown at the top of the billing and subscription section.

HOW TO ENTER AN OPENING BALANCE FOR THE CHART OF ACCOUNTS.

The chart of accounts is a list of all your company's accounts as well as their balances. When using QuickBooks, you can use these accounts to categorize your sales forms into reports and tax forms. Each account has a transaction history and is divided into several smaller accounts to make record-keeping easier for the user. QuickBooks automatically calculates your profit and loss accounts as you enter transactions into the system. This accounting feature consists of four major components: expense accounts, liabilities, income, and assets.

Here are the steps for entering an opening balance for the chart accounts:

1. In the left-hand menu, click *Accounting*.
2. Click *Charts of Accounts* at the top of the page.
3. Scroll to the account you wish to set and select *Edit* in the dropdown menu.
4. Enter the balance amount and the date you wish to apply, save, and close.

EDITING AN OPENING BALANCE FOR THE CHART OF ACCOUNTS

1. Navigate to *Settings* and then to *Chart of Accounts*.
2. Locate the account and then click *View Registration*.
3. Locate the balance entry that represents the opening balance. To find the opening balance item, sort the date column from latest to oldest.
4. Click *Opening Balance Entry*.
5. Adjust the amount.
6. Click *Save*.

RESETTING PASSWORDS

In case you are unable to log into your account:

1. Go to http://account.intuit.com/
2. Click *Sign In* at the top right.

3. Enter your sign-in credentials (email address and password), and you will go to the login page (www.qbo.intuit.com), scroll down just a bit, and click *Forgot my User ID or Password.*
4. Enter your phone number, email, or user ID to receive a code.
5. After entering the information that QuickBooks needs to reset your password, click on *Reset.*
6. Key in the 6-digit code sent to your email or phone, depending on your choice. When prompted to replace your security question, just click *Okay.*
7. Complete the following prompts to retrieve your password or reset it.

HOW TO CHANGE YOUR COMPANY SETTINGS

The Company tab allows you to view information such as the company's name, address, contact information, and Employer Identification Number (EIN). Adjustments may be made to meet both users' and customers' needs on the accounts. These changes can be made from various tabs, including Billing & Subscription, Usage, Sales, Expenses, Payments, Time, and Advanced. You can change your company's settings by following the steps outlined below.

To change settings:

1. Click *Settings.*
2. Navigate to the *Account and Settings* section.
3. Click on a tab.
4. In a section, click *Edit.*
5. Choose an item to edit. A field emerges, prompting you to make changes, then save.
6. Click *Done* to save your changes.

HOW TO RECORD A JOURNAL ENTRY

Accounting journals are necessary because they track how money is spent; it would be difficult to determine where funds were spent without them. Accounting may appear to be the last thing you want to do while running a small business, but it's not complex mathematics; rather, it is the process of capturing and logically presenting financial data. Journaling is the same thing.

1. Click the *New* button to access the accounting field for new entries.

2. Click on the *Journal Entry* tab.
3. Select an account depending on credit or debit needs, then key in the data in the appropriate column and format.
4. Depending on the choice of the transaction, enter the same amount on the opposite side, either credit or debit the account. Countercheck to ensure both the credit column and the debit column balance on one line.
5. In the note area, provide the reason for the journal entry.
6. Click *Save* and close.

| CHAPTER 3 |

BILLS AND EXPENSES

| HOW TO MANAGE EXPENSES

I f expenses have been paid in full, they should be recorded. Bills should be included if you plan to pay them off later.

Since you've already paid for them, you can change the costs you've added in QuickBooks at any time. Any changes you make will be reflected in the invoice you send them if you choose to charge.

1. Go to Expenses.
2. Find the expense you want to edit.

3. Select *Edit* or view in the *Action* column.
4. Update the transaction as required.
5. Select *Save* and close.

HOW TO RECORD CHEQUES

Any expense can be paid with a cheque and tracked using expense accounts and non-stock, service, or charge items.

1. From the navigator, click *Banking and Credit Cards*, then click *Cheques* or from the *Chart of Accounts* window, select the *Activities* menu, then choose *Write Cheques*.
2. In the *Bank Account* field, choose your current account.
3. In *Pay the Order of*, choose from the dropdown list.
4. Enter the amount in the cheque.
5. Input the address and memo fields.
6. Edit items that are displayed from your purchase order or enter new ones.
7. To enter shipping charges and any other expenses not associated with any one item, click the *Expenses* tab, enter each charge, and connect it with the correct expense account.
8. Record the cheque.

Recording A Cheque

How to write a cheque on an "Income by Customer Summary" report:

1. Click *Banking* at the menu bar and select *Write Cheques*.
2. Select the appropriate bank account.
3. Select a *Payee* in the pay to the order.
4. Filter the date and the cheque number correctly.
5. Select *Expense Account*, then input the amount at the *Expense* Tab.
6. Click *Save* and close.

Printing a Cheque

1. From the *File* menu, choose *Print Form*, and then choose *Print Cheques*.

2. From the bank account dropdown list, choose the current account that contains the cheques you want to print
3. Check that the number in the first cheque number field matches the first number on your printer's cheques.
4. Select the cheques you want to print.
5. Click *Okay.*
6. To print duplicate copies of vouchers cheques, input two in the number of copies field, then click *Print.*

HOW TO DELETE A BILL

You can void or delete a cheque from the "Cheque" page so that you can review the details in the original transaction.

1. Go to *Expenses.*
2. On the Expenses tab, select Filter.
3. In the Type field, select Cheque.
4. Select the date range in which the cheque was received and select Apply.
5. To open the Cheque list screen, select the cheque to void from the Expense Transactions list.
6. Select More and select Void from the menu.
7. Click the Yes option to confirm the voiding of the cheque.

Voiding a Cheque Without Opening the Transaction

You can void a cheque from the Expense Transactions list without opening the transaction.

1. Go to *Expenses.*
2. In the *Expense Transactions* list, search the cheque to void.
3. Select *Void* from the *View* or *Edit* on the drop-down menu.
4. Select *Yes* to confirm that you want to void the cheque.

HOW TO DELETE AN EXPENSE

1. Go to *Expenses.*
2. Find the expense you want to delete.

3. Select the *View or Edit* dropdown in the Action column
4. Select *Delete*.
5. Click *Yes* to confirm transaction deletion.

| HOW TO SET UP BULK PAYMENTS

1. Go to *Charts of Accounts.*
2. Select the bank account you will be making payments from.
3. Once you have selected the bank account, click on the account history, and select *Edit.*
4. A new field called *Create Batch Payment* will be displayed at the bottom of the screen. Select the field.
5. Enter your bank details; some banks might also need a direct entry user ID. If it is required, add the entry.
6. Click *Save.*
7. Go to the *Suppliers* tab.
8. Select the supplier you need to pay.
9. Record the details of the supplier you intend to pay by clicking on the edit button next to the supplier's name.
10. Select *Create batch payment box.*
11. Fill in the account name and number.
12. Click *Save.*
13. Click on the *Add Button* at the top of the screen and select pay bill. Add amount to be paid and mark to pay.
14. Click on *Create a Bulk Payment.*
15. Save the file.

| HOW TO RECORD A CASH EXPENSE

Expenses: An expense is the cost of operations that a company incurs to generate revenue during its operations. If a business meets the IRS guidelines, it can deduct tax-deductible expenses on its income tax returns. Accountants record expenses using one of two methods: cash or accrual.

Recording an Expense in QuickBooks

1. Select Add New.
2. Select Expenses.

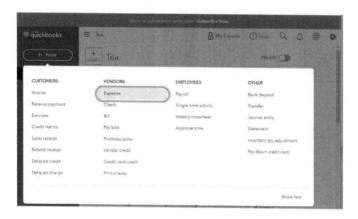

1. Select the supplier in the Payee field. The payment section also accounts for transactions made via bank for easy access and retrieval.
2. Input the date for the expense in the Payment Date Area.
3. Choose the payment method for the expense in the Mode of Payment field. Enter the expenditure information in the Category Details section. Select the cost account you use to monitor spending transactions from the Category section. Then, write a description for it. You may also insert items and services in the item details box to categorize the expenditure.
4. Enter the taxable amount.
5. Select the Billable option and input the customer's name in the Customer field.
6. When finished, choose Save and exit.
7. The Memo field also accepts notes. These show on reports and in the account history. If you utilize expenditure vouchers, choose Print to get a printed copy.

HOW TO MANAGE BILLS

Bills: This is the amount of money you owe your suppliers.

There are two ways you can manage your bills:

- Pay your bills as soon as you receive them. Write a cheque and assign their amounts to the appropriate expense account.
- Pay your bills later. You can enter the bills into your accounts payable account and set a reminder to remind you when they are due.

How to Enter Bills

1. From the activity's menu, click *Enter Bills* to display the enter bills window
2. In the *Supplier or Vendor* field, choose the vendor and the existing purchase orders that will be displayed
3. Select *Yes* to receive against one or more purchase orders.
4. On the *Open Purchase Orders* window, click each purchase order containing items you have received and are billed for. Click *Okay*.
5. Change the date of the bill. This is optional.
6. Enter the amount on the bill.
7. Input the reference number, terms, and memo fields as needed.
8. Click the *Items* tab. You can edit items entered from your purchase order or enter a new one.

9. To enter shipping charges or taxes not associated with any one item, click the *Expenses* tab, enter each charge, and associate it with the correct expense account
10. Use the *Split VAT or Add-on* buttons to change the VAT amount on each line of the detail area. This is also optional.
11. Record the bill.

How to Edit Bills and Payments

1. From the list's menu, go to *Chart of Accounts* and click the *Accounts Payable* account.
2. Find the specific bill or payments.
3. Click *Edit* and make the changes required.
4. Click *Okay* to save.

How to Pay Bills

1. Click Pay Bills from the activity's menu to display the pay bills tab.
2. Choose the type of payment and the account from which you want to pay the bill.
3. Fill in the optional fields in the pay bills window.
4. Select the bill to pay by ticking the checkbox.
5. To pay only part of the bill, enter the amount you would like to pay toward this billing in the amount paid column.
6. Record the payment.

How to Apply a Credit

1. Click the *Purchases and Vendors* tab from the navigator, then click *Enter Bills*.
2. At the top of the enter bills window, click *Credit*.
3. Enter the amount of the credit.
4. Enter the expense accounts or customers to which you want to assign the credit
5. Use the *Split VAT or Add-on* buttons to change the VAT amount on each line of the detail area.
6. Record credit.

How to Enter a Bill When You Receive It

1. Select the *Purchase and Vendor* tab from the navigator tab, then choose the *Receive Bill* icon.
2. Enter the vendor's name and press the tab in the item receipt window.
3. Click the item receipt connected with the bill and click *Okay*.
4. Complete the reference #, terms, and memo fields.
5. Correct the amounts if necessary.
6. Make sure the amount shown in the amount field is the same as the total on the bill.
7. Record the bill.

HOW TO SET UP EXPENSE SETTINGS

Setting Up Expenses Settings

1. Click on the Add icon or Create Menu from the top menu bar.
2. Select the Expenses option under supplier.
3. Open expenses.
4. Enter the supplier's name in the payee field and click Add. You can either input the name of a person or a business. If there are multiple expenses in your transaction, you can leave this field blank.
5. Choose a payee.
6. Click on Add Details to input additional information like the type of currency and supplier or vendor, select Save if you choose to do it later.
7. Add details.
8. Choose a Payment Account from which the money of purchase will be deducted. Always put in mind that if you are using a debit card for the transaction, you must choose a Cheque Account, even if the card has a Visa on it.
9. Choose an account.
10. Input the date of purchase in the Payment Date field.
11. Enter the date.
12. Select how you made the payment in the Payment Method field – by credit card, cheque, or cash.
13. Choose payment method.
14. Under Account, you need to choose a category for the purchase you have made.

15. Choose a category. If you cannot find the appropriate category for any item, you can add a new category and amount by clicking on the Add Lines option.
16. Add Description.
17. In the Amount field, enter the amount of purchased item and, if applicable, add the appropriate tax in the Tax field.
18. Add Amount.
19. If you want to create another expense, click on Save and New or select Save and Close upon completion.

* Some options to consider that will assist you in tracking expenses before you Save and Close:

The Billable column appears if you have enabled the billable expense tracking feature. Mark the Billable column and enter the customer's name. You have the option of enabling this feature for specific clients. Go to Accounts and Settings, then the Expenses tab to perform this option.

Note: If you received credit for an expense billed to a customer in the past, make sure to mention that customer on credit and check the Billable box as well. If this is not done, the customer will be charged for the expenses on the next invoice, and no credit will be issued.

- If you want to see an income or the expense report for each customer, you should run an income by Customer Summary Report.
- You should add a brief note or Memo in case you want it to be on reports that include the purchase or in the Account History.

HOW TO MAKE EXPENSES BILLABLE

To record billable expenses, turn on the billable expense tracking.

1. Click on the *Settings* menu.
2. Select *Account and settings*.
3. Navigate to the Expenses tab.
4. Select *Edit* at the Bills and expenses section.
5. Press the *Show Items* table on expense and purchase forms.
6. Track expenses/items by the client.

7. Make expenses and items billable by setting up the Markup rate, Billable expense, tracking, Sales, tax charge, and Bill payment terms.
8. Select *Save.*
9. Input a billable expense.

How to Charge a Client for A Cost

1. Click on New.
2. Select the *Bill, Expense, or Check* transaction.
3. Choose a payee.
4. In the *Classification* section, choose the expenditure account.
5. Enter the expense's description and amount, then check **Billable**.
6. In the client column, click the customer to charge.
7. Tick the *Tax* checkbox or specify a tax if you wish to charge tax.
8. Save and exit.

Expenses to Invoices

1. Link the chargeable expenditure to the customer's Invoice.
2. Select *New*.
3. Select *Invoice.*
4. Select the client for whom you made a chargeable expenditure. Add to invoice window opens.
5. Add the billable expenditure to your customer.
6. Save and exit.

CHAPTER 4

INVOICING AND QUOTING TUTORIALS

HOW TO CREATE AN INVOICE IN QUICKBOOKS

How do you get paid for the goods and services you offer? After-sales, you may want to send an invoice to your customers. Simply include the products or services you are selling on an invoice and email it to your client. QuickBooks facilitates this transaction by creating invoices for each transactional activity in your company.

The following are the steps for creating an invoice:

1. Create an invoice from scratch.
2. Select the *Create Invoices* option on the *Customers* menu.

3. Select a customer or customer job from the dropdown menu.
4. Select *Add New* to include customers not listed.
5. Input the relevant information at the top of the form.
6. Select the item(s) in the detail field.

Create a Discount Item

1. Go to the *Lists* menu on the home screen.
2. Click on the *Item List* option.
3. Select *New*.
4. Select *Type Discount* from the dropdown menu.
5. Input an item name or number and a brief description of the product or service.
6. Enter the discount amount and/or percentage in the amount field.
7. Choose the income account you want to use to track discounts you give to customers from the account dropdown menu.
8. Click on *Tax Code* for the item.
9. Select *Okay*, *Save*, then *Close*.

CREATING AND SENDING AN INVOICE IN QUICKBOOKS

Creating and sending an invoice is the foundation of any transaction because customers and small business owners must share the details for accounting purposes and customer payment processing. The steps for creating and sending invoices in QuickBooks are as follows:

1. Click on *Create Invoices* on the homepage or the customer menu on the QuickBooks dashboard.
2. Click on the *Job* tab on the customer menu, then choose customer option for estimate window to appear.
3. Select *Estimate* to be included in the invoice
4. Then, click *Save* and close.

EDITING AN INVOICE IN QUICKBOOKS

It's possible to make mistakes during the entry process. To change or edit an invoice, follow the steps outlined below:

1. Click on the *Invoice* you wish to edit.
2. Choose the *Edit* options dropdown from the invoices box.
3. Delete the existing payment on QBO before pushing the updated invoice.

HOW TO CUSTOMIZE AN INVOICE IN QUICKBOOKS

A personalized invoice allows you to sell your company and promote your brand. The invoice logo represents your company's brand and appears on all transaction forms in QuickBooks Online. Because your logo will be created outside of QBO, keep the following factors in mind when designing yours. The logo should be as follows:

1. A gif, bmp, png, jpg, jpe, or jpeg file less than 10 MB in size.
2. Bit depth of twenty-four bits or less (or color depth).
3. Either square or round.

Customizing an invoice, assigning tax codes to goods, assigning pricing to things, generating an item for a product, and documenting hardware and software purchases inventories are some of the most common modifications in the QuickBooks system.

These changes are affected by the following steps:

1. To begin, go to the *Gear* icon in the top right-hand corner.
2. Choose *Custom Form Styles* from the *Your Company* dropdown menu.
3. Choose *Invoice* from the *New Style* dropdown menu. This panel has three tabs: Design, Content, and Emails.

Design – This is where you can change or add your logo, as well as your font and color scheme.

Content – This is where you can change your content, add a website/address, and change the label sizes.

Emails – This is where you can choose whether to show complete or partial data and write a note for your client. Most of your work will be stored in the *Content* tab.

You can customize what information appears in your header in the first editing area. Mark any of the boxes to remove a field.

In the middle section, you can change the columns, add items, and add descriptions. You can also display the total amount owed to a client and payments and credits.

You can customize the third party with a statement and tagline and any discount, deposit, or estimate options.

Finally, double-check that the email you sent matches the invoice you received. This invoice template is now finished and ready to use. Each option is described in detail to easily create a professional invoice.

| HOW TO DELETE AN INVOICE IN QUICKBOOKS

An invoice may need to be deleted if it has been duplicated or if the transactions have been canceled for various reasons. The following is the procedure for deleting an invoice:

1. Click on the *Sales* or *Expenses* menu to find the transaction.
2. Click on the dropdown tab and choose *View* or *Edit* to access the transactions.
3. You can also add the reasons for the deletion or cancellation on the memo area then save the details.
4. Click on "more" in the footer, then click on "delete."
5. Click *Yes* to initiate the changes.

| HOW TO PRINT AN INVOICE IN QUICKBOOKS

Invoices can be printed for distribution to customers or financial reporting. If this is the case, follow the steps below to create a copy.

1. Select *Reports* on the panel on the left.
2. Type *Transactions List by Vendor* in the search bar.
3. Click on the correct date under the *Report* period.
4. Select *Run Report* to print.

HOW TO SET UP AUTO-INVOICE REMINDERS

If a customer does not pay an invoice by the due date, they are reminded via invoice reminders. When you enable invoice reminders for the first time, default reminders are set. You can change or remove these reminders to meet your organization's needs.

To set up automatic invoice reminders:

1. Navigate to the *Account and Settings* menu under *Settings*.
2. Click the *Sales* tab.
3. Select *Edit* from the *Reminders* menu.
4. Activate the *Automatic Invoice Reminders* feature.
5. Choose *Reminder 1* from the menu and flip it on.
6. Specify the days and times before or after from the dropdown menu. There is a 90-day grace period for sending invoice reminder emails.
7. You may add more reminders as necessary.
8. After enabling reminders, you may modify the message. Note that you may adjust each reminder's email template to meet the preset dates.
9. Edit the topic line as required in the *Subject* line area.
10. To customize your welcome, tick the *Use Email Greeting* option. Choose an appropriate salutation from the provided menus.
11. In the email message field, delete the text and write your own. You may also use the standard message.
12. After that, tap *Save* and *Done*.

HOW TO MANAGE OVERDUE INVOICES IN QUICKBOOKS

A consistent flow of funds in and out is critical in any company to enable smooth day-to-day operations. Unpaid invoices can cause a slew of problems for your business. The first step in informing your customers that they have a payment obligation is to send them past-due notices. Another strategy for assisting your customers in making timely payments is to offer them online payment options.

The steps for dealing with past-due debts are outlined below:

1. Click on the *Customer* menu.
2. Choose *Receiving Payments*.
3. Select the client from the dropdown menu under *Received From*.

4. Set the amount to be settled by adding it in the *Payment Amount* area.
5. Save and exit the program.
6. Click on the *Okay* button to continue.

❙ HOW TO TRACK BILLABLE TIME IN QUICKBOOKS

If you bill by the hour or pay people based on the number of hours they work, tracking billable time is ideal. In this instance:

1. Enter the job as a *Sub-customer* of the customer to track billable time.
2. Click the *Sale* or *Invoice* tab to choose the customer.
3. Select *New* customer.
4. Enter all the appropriate details for the *Sub-customer*.
5. Click *Sub-customer Check Box*.
6. Select the parent customer in the *Parent Customer* dropdown menu.
7. Click the *Bill* button with a parent.
8. Select *Save*.

Activate Billable Time

1. Select *Account Settings* from the dropdown menu under *Settings*.
2. Select the *Time* tab from the dropdown menu.
3. In the timesheet, choose *Edit* from the context menu.
4. Select *Allow Time to be Billable* from the menu.
5. To allow users to observe billable rates, click the *Show Billing Rate for Users Entering the Time* option when entering the time.
6. Click *Save*, then click *Done* to complete the process.

Recording Billable Time

1. Click on the *Time* tab, then select *Time Entries*.
2. Choose the *Add Time* option and the appropriate user.
3. Customize the date ranges, then choose the day(s) entries are done for.
4. Input the hours worked or press the *Start and End Date* tab to add the date ranges.
5. Select *Add Work* details, then select the client or the project from the dropdown menu.

CHAPTER 5

SALES AND RECEIPTS

HOW TO RECORD A REFUND

The customer's money should be refunded, and the books should be balanced to ensure that the transaction's reflections are documented. This section explains how to record a refund based on various factors, such as whether the client has paid or issued the invoice to the correct individual.

1. To begin, click *New* and then *Credit Memo*.
2. Select a suitable client in the customer field.

3. Add the credit memo, date of amount, tax, and product or service (if applicable).
4. Close it by clicking *Save*.
5. Assuming the consumer has overpaid, the credit message is unneeded.
6. Select *Expense* from the *New* dropdown menu.
7. Enter the appropriate client in the *Payee* section.
8. In the Payment account area, pick the refunding bank.
9. Select the debtor's account in the *Category* section
10. Enter the refund amount in the *Amount* field.
11. Select the applicable tax in the *Tax Box*, including the inclusive and exclusive tax.
12. To save your work, click *Save*.
13. Then, choose to receive money from the *New* menu.
14. Fill in the payment method and a deposit amount for the client. The balance should be zero since they cancel each other.
15. Click *Save* and close it.
16. Match the record found in your online banking for verification

Refund for Paid Bills

1. Select "New", then pick "Client Credit" from the dropdown option.
2. Input the payment date, amount, tax, and category columns for the transactions you will get credit.
3. Select "Save" and then click "Close".
4. Add the payee, choose the "Client Credit", and deposit methods from the dropdown menus.

Credit Card Refunds

1. Click *New* and then *Credit Card* from the dropdown menu.
2. Choose the applicable client in the *Payee* field.
3. Input the payment date, the amount of the refund, the tax, and the category.
4. Choose *Save and Finish* to complete your refund.

HOW TO CREATE A RECEIPT

QuickBooks can create and track sales receipts. You can provide customers with an immediate sales receipt when you charge customers for future remittances. This QuickBooks feature reduces errors, saves time, and reduces the likelihood of recurring conflicts. It saves time by eliminating the need to enter receipt data twice. Here's how to make a receipt in QuickBooks:

1. Click the *New* tab from the dropdown list.
2. Click either the *Refund Receipt* or the *Give Refund* options from the dropdown menu.
3. Choose the client to be repaid from the dropdown menu by clicking on the *Customer* option.
4. Click the *Refund* option
5. Select the bank into which payments were deposited from the dropdown option.
6. Add all returning items or services to the *Product or Service* column.
7. Fill in the appropriate boxes for the date, quantity, rate, amount, and tax, then click *Save* and close.

HOW TO RECEIVE A PAYMENT

Using a sales receipt or a bank deposit to pay an invoice counts revenue twice but leaves the invoice unpaid. As a result, collection operations may become ineffective, and client relationships deteriorate. Receiving payments and adjusting amounts in accounting is just as important as collecting money. Follow these steps to ensure that payments are received and that the charts of accounts are accurate.

1. To access, click the *Receive Payment* button.
2. At the top of the left menu bar, click the *New* button.
3. Under *Customers*, choose *Receive Payment* in the top column. It's critical to apply the received money to the relevant customer invoice.
4. To find the correct invoice, choose the client in the top-right corner of the receiving payment page. Choose the client from whom you got money.
5. Enter the date you received your payment in payment date bar.
6. Choose between a cheque or cash as your payment option through which your customer sends you a payment from payment method bar.

7. On Reference No. bar provide the cheque number, or leave it blank if cash received.
8. If this is the only check to be deposited in your bank account, you can select the appropriate bank account. However, if this check will be combined with other checks or cash, then you should record the payment received in Undeposited Funds.
9. Enter the total amount of cash or cheques received.
10. Enter the percentage of the total cash collected in "F" that will be applied to each invoice mentioned in "G".
11. Click the green *Save and Close* button to save the transaction.
12. Hover over *Sales* after selecting *Customers* from the left menu.
13. Locate the client whose payment you logged and click on their name.
14. Check to see whether the invoice for which payment was received has been recorded as "Paid."
15. Check that the payment is indicated as "Closed." If payment is displayed as "Open," it has not been properly applied to an invoice.

| CHAPTER 6 |

BANK ACCOUNTS

| HOW TO CONNECT TO YOUR BANK ACCOUNT

With the current digitization of the banking industry, most transactions are done online, with banks embracing this technology to keep up with the current dynamics and ensure a wider reach. QuickBooks' features and settings allow you to connect to your bank accounts and monitor transactions as they occur.

1. On the homepage's "Bank Accounts" section, click *Connect an Account*.
2. Select a bank and a username and password for account access.
3. When finished, click *Log In*. Once connected, you will get a list of all your bank accounts.

4. Select the business account and notify QuickBooks of its existence. QuickBooks will download all transactions for the preceding 90 days with a single click.

5. Choose the *Category* or *Match* column on the *Bank and Credit Cards* tab to sort the transactions.

6. Click it to see the dropdown details for the first transaction in the list.

7. To re-categorize a transaction, use the transaction menu. Click *Add* in the column on the right.

8. Choose *Payee*. Click *Add New* to add a new payee to the menu.

9. Enter the new payee's name and click *Save*. After that, you may fill in the blanks.

10. Open the transaction and choose *Transfer*. Purchases from various categories can be divided.

11. In the *Split Transaction* box, choose the relevant categories and their respective amounts.

12. Go to *Batch Actions* and click *Accept* to accept all of them.

13. Click *In QuickBooks*, pick the transaction, and undo any wrong entries, if there are any. Once in *New Transactions*, you can move it.

HOW TO IMPORT A SPREADSHEET OF TRANSACTIONS

In this case, we'll assume you used a personal credit card for both personal and business expenses. You then downloaded the transactions from your credit card company as an Excel document and deleted all non-business-related transactions. You will be given an Excel file (spreadsheet) containing business transactions that you can import into QuickBooks. The steps for importing are as follows:

1. Remove any extraneous data from the excel file to clean it up.

2. To make the XLS file readable by QuickBooks, convert it to CVS format by choosing *File* and *Save As* and setting the file type to CSV.

3. Select the account the file is to be added to.

4. To upload the file, go to the *Accounts* page and click on the account to be added.

5. In the top right-hand corner of the screen, click the downward-pointing arrow next to the *Updated* button.

6. Select the *File Upload* option from the dropdown menu.

7. On the next page, QuickBooks will ask you where you got your data from, whether it's a file on your computer or an upload directly from your financial institution.

8. Select the QuickBooks account where you want to upload the bank file. It's not always necessary to assign an existing registration; you can always *Add New* and create a new account for your needs.

9. The data in each column should be interpreted and mapped into a transaction. Each QuickBooks transaction has a date column, and so does each transaction in the Excel spreadsheet. QuickBooks includes a description box as well. Column 4, *Memo*, is the closest match to the description box. Finally, and most importantly, the amount of the transaction.

10. Distinguish between the two types of bank transactions. Separate payments and deposits into separate columns. Remember that banks may combine all statistics into one column and use negative and positive values.

11. On the following page, click *Next,* and QuickBooks will display all transaction data as it has been interpreted. You'll see the matching dates, descriptions, and sums, and if everything looks correct, you can continue with the import by clicking *Next.*

12. Verify the transactions.

HOW TO SET UP A DIRECT BANK FEED

Direct feeds connect your bank account to QuickBooks safely and dependably. With a Direct Feed, QuickBooks can accept transactions without requiring you to enter your bank's sign-in credentials.

The following are the steps for enrolling in a direct bank feed:

1. Go to *Banking Area.*
2. Click the *Link Account* option in the top-right corner of the screen.
3. Enter your bank's name into the search field and click on it.
4. Select the *Get Direct Bank Feeds* option and create a Client Authority Form.

CHAPTER 7

GST AND BAS

G ST is a tax on goods and services delivered or sold by an individual or small business organization.

Individuals collect taxes when they sell things, and they pay taxes when they buy products and services from other individuals and corporations.

QuickBooks can automatically calculate GST on your receipts and invoices for simple and accurate filings. When first using QuickBooks, you'll need to configure how and where you'll be charging GST.

Here's how to get everything all set up and running.

SET UP AND USE GST:

Follow the instructions below to set up tax:

1. Go to Taxes and click Set up tax.

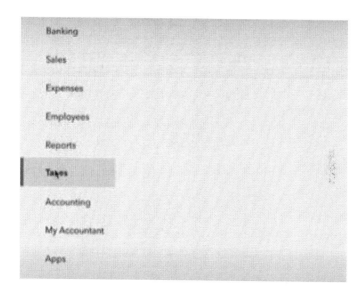

2. Enter the following information: tax name, description, and tax agency name.

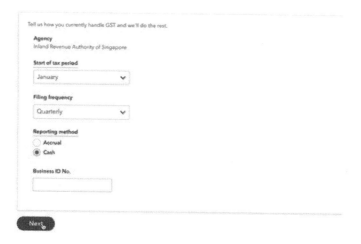

3. Enter your Business ID (optional).
4. Choose the start of the current tax period.
5. Choose your tax filing frequency.
6. Choose your Reporting Method (typically Accrual, except if you're a professional service provider). Please consult your consultant if you are unsure).
7. Enter the sales rate, then click: This tax is levied on purchases, if applicable.
8. Select Next, followed by OK.

After you've established the tax center, you may add custom tax rates.

Note: Depending on where you live, QuickBooks may already have taxes set up for you.

BAS

The Business Activity Statement (BAS) is used to record and pay GST, Pay As You Go (PAYG) Instalments, PAYG withholding tax, and other tax requirements.

It can be filed once per month or once every three months; most QuickBooks users it will be the quarterly option.

The timely submission of your Business Activity Statement (BAS) is an important aspect of running a small business. When cash flow is tight, no one wants to make late payments.

Failure to file will result in fines and additional fees.

QuickBooks helps you automate your GST tracking and keep accurate records.

Let's have a look at the GST Centre in your client's QuickBooks.

Using a GST Prepare BAS:

1. First, You have to log into your client's QuickBooks by clicking on the QB icon.

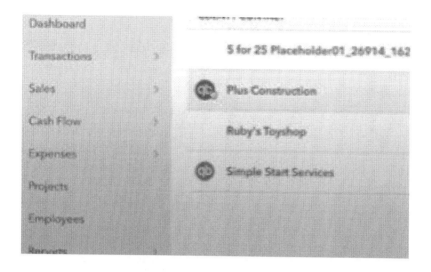

2. To access the GST Centre, click the GST tab in the left-hand navigation.

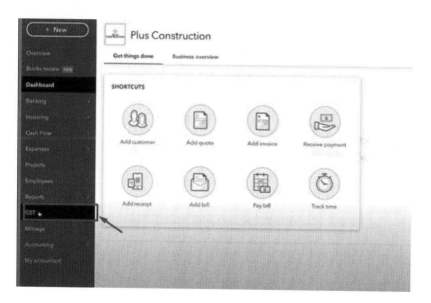

3. Once inside, the first thing you want to do is set up the tax settings.

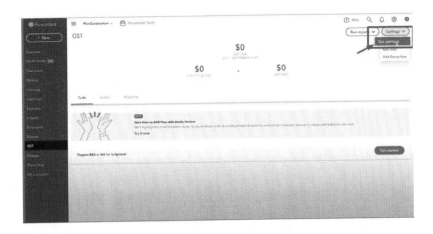

4. You can select which taxes apply the lodge man frequency and the accounting method used.

5. You can also turn on PAYG instalments as well as other taxes.

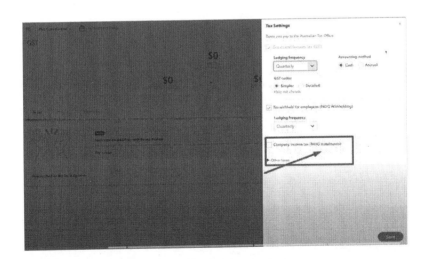

6. Once you are happy with the tax settings to complete a BAS, simply click the get started button.

Your one-stop shop for everything BAS

Let's set up BAS so we can calculate GST and other obligations, prepare for lodgment, and you can even lodge BAS without leaving QuickBooks.

7. Here you can select the date range for the first because you were lodging.

8. Once done, the GST Centre will automatically calculate the GST on sales and purchases for the period.
9. The next page will calculate your PAYG obligations, which is pulled from QuickBooks payroll, and the final page will give you a full summary for your final review, which you can then Mark has lodged in QuickBooks.

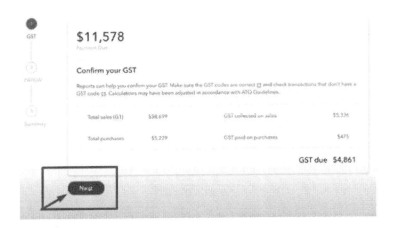

10. You can then visit the website to lodge the bass.
11. Once you were done, you will see the BOSU lodged under the To Pay section.

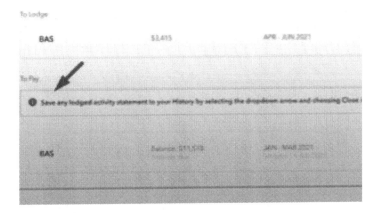

12. To mark it as paid. Click the record payment button and enter the repayment amount and date.

13. This will create a transaction to the relevant GST and PAYG accounts, with the balance showing in the ATO clearing account to be matched to the bank transaction from your bank feed.

14. Once you mark BAS as paid, it will move to the payments tab, and your next BAS due will show under the To Do Tab to help with reviewing the numbers for your bus.

15. You have access to a range of reports within the centre, such as the transactions without GST report and transactions by tax code.

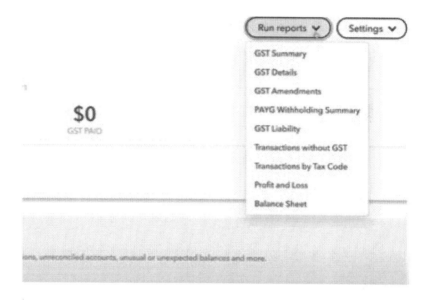

That's it. You are ready to start using the GST centre for your client's accounts.

HOW TO SET UP GST TRACKING AND BAS E-LODGMENT

The dashboard monitors and summarizes GST-recorded QuickBooks transactions. This provides a quick summary of how much you owe the tax office during a specific time period. GST Rates are QuickBooks Online default settings used to code the applicable GST tax against your transaction.

Set up a GST tracking and BAS e-lodgment system by following the steps below.

1. Click *GST Centre* from the left-hand side navigation bar.

2. Compare your BAS figures to the report, BAS summary, BAS details, and amendment details.
3. Click on *GST* from the left menu.
4. Select *Prepare BAS Link* under the *Next BAS to Lodge* section.
5. The BAS window will open a BAS fields based on the values recorded against the Tax Codes for the selected period. During preparation, some fields may necessitate direct insertion.
6. Click *Record to Reveal* from the left-hand menu for adjustments.
7. Click *Mark as Lodged* and complete the BAS period.

| HOW TO PREPARE AND LODGE YOUR BAS

Other than the GST, some businesses are required to report taxes. PAYG withholding and PAYG income tax installments are the most common additional taxes. Fringe benefits, fuel taxes, and luxury contexts are other taxes that can be reported. By enabling the GST setup, you can report additional taxes. You can also enable them while accumulating GST or changing the GST settings. To enable in settings, follow the steps below:

1. Select Prepare BAS from the GST menu. If it is the first BAS for this firm in QuickBooks, choose Get Started.
2. Depending on QuickBooks transactions, QuickBooks will provide total sales (including GST), GST collected on sales, total purchases, and GST paid on purchases. If all seems to be in order, click Next.
3. Check your total wages paid and total tax withheld statistics in QuickBooks if you've implemented PAYG Withholding. Then click Next.
4. Enter your Income Tax instalment amount if you've activated PAYG Instalments in QuickBooks. Then click Next.
5. Enter the amount owed if you've enabled FBT, fuel tax credits, Luxury car tax, or wine equalisation tax in QuickBooks. Then click Next.
6. After reading the whole activity statement, choose Mark as lodged in QuickBooks to finish the tax period.
7. After the lodgement, lodge your BAS.
8. After you've made the payment, keep track of it in QuickBooks.

CHAPTER 8

STAFF AND PAYROLL

HOW TO SET UP PAYROLL IN QUICKBOOKS

I f you already use QuickBooks Online and need to pay staff, consider adding QuickBooks Payroll to your membership package. It is accessible from the same system that you use to handle your company's books, allowing for the smooth transfer of payroll costs to the relevant general ledger accounts.

Setting up employee payroll in QuickBooks is simple; employees can not only view and download their pay stubs, but they can also enter their own information.

All that is required is to send them an email inviting them to log in and enter information about the activity they have completed or the workforce before they are set up in QuickBooks.

Below are the steps to set up Payrolls:

1. Log in to QuickBooks Online.
2. From the left menu bar, click Payroll, then Overview.

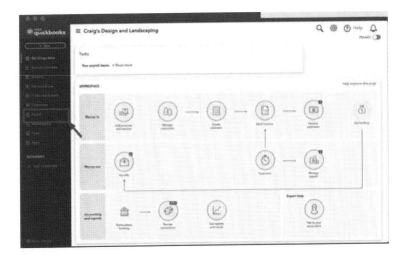

1. If this is your first time setting up payroll, the Get Started option will show; click on it.
2. Fill in the needed information by following the on-screen directions.
   - The date of your next paycheck (or the date you want to begin paying your team in QuickBooks)
   - The actual location where all or the majority of your workers work
   - The name, email address, and phone number of the payroll contact. This is the primary person in charge of paying your team.
3. After you have completed the Business information section, you may begin adding your first employee.

HOW TO ADD EMPLOYEES

Gathering basic information on your workers, such as their name, pay info, direct deposit info, date of birth, and current contact information etc., is necessary before you begin.

4. Select Payroll from the menu on the left, then click Employees.
5. Click Add an employee.

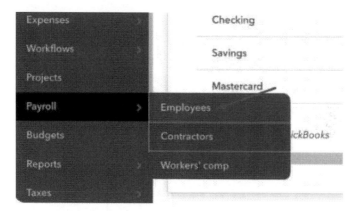

6. Add the name and email address of your employee. Make sure Employee self-setup is enabled if you want them to submit their own personal, tax, and banking information. QuickBooks will send them an invitation to QuickBooks Workforce automatically. Your employee may provide their address, SSN, W-4, and banking information.

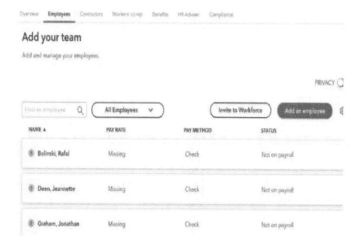

7. Once all of the information has been entered, click Add employee.

8. Select any box to enter the remaining personnel information.
   - You will not be able to alter some data on the Personal details, Tax withholding, or Payment method cards if employee self-setup is enabled. If you wish to change those tabs, go to Personal Info and uncheck Employee self-setup.

9. When you're finished adding information to a tab, click Save.

| HOW TO PROCESS A PAY RUN

After you've finished configuring payroll in QuickBooks, you may begin processing your first pay run. Now comes the exciting part: paying your employees! A pay run only needs to be set once for the date part, after which all subsequent pay runs will be moved to the next pay date period.

1. Go to the main payroll screen and click *Run Pay Roll*.

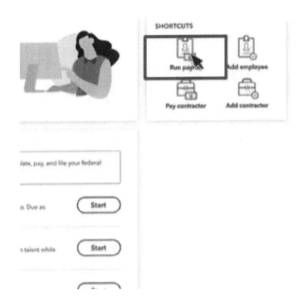

2. Once you open the pay run screen, select *Pay Schedule*. Input the date for the pay period ending and when the pay run is paid, then click *Create*.

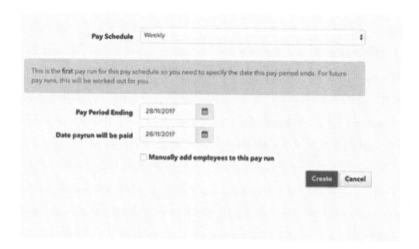

3. The next screen displays a summary of all employees in that run, including tax and their salaries or earnings. By clicking on the individual employee, you can view more information about them.

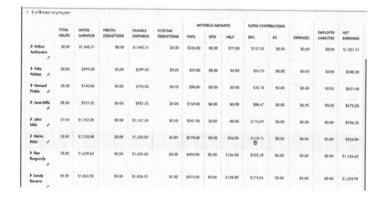

4. The action button is important because it allows you to make additional selections to correct or amend the employee pay run.

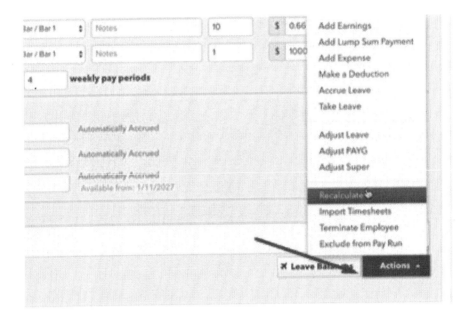

5. Check that you have chosen the right bank account, pay month, and pay date. You can also make changes as needed.
6. Change the employee's pay method as appropriate.
7. If relevant, enter the number of hours worked. TIP: To hide or reveal pay types, click the Settings button below the TOTAL PAY.
8. Select Payroll Preview.
9. After filling in the information needed, click *Save* and note any prompt alerts for an action.
10. To amend or preview a specific cheque, click the Edit icon next to the net pay, then click OK when finished.

11. To finish the pay run, click on *Finalize Pay Run* and verify that the date paid is correct, then click *Finalize*.

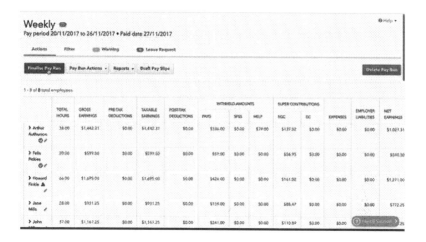

12. Payslips can be sent to employees quickly using the payslip option.
13. You're ready to go! Select Print paycheques, then Finish payroll to print paycheques.
14. After it has been finalized, the pay run is now locked. Only before any bank statements are processed can they be unlocked and changed.
15. Once the pay run is complete, download the files that will be uploaded to the bank, run any payroll reports, and send payslips.

HOW TO CREATE TIMESHEETS, LEAVE, AND EXPENSES FOR EMPLOYEES

Creating Employee's Timesheets

Employees who are required to use timesheets will be able to view, create, and delete timesheets on their own from within the Work Zone app.

Employees must use timesheets in the employee details, Pay Run defaults page, Payroll Settings, and Employee Portal Settings if they want to access timesheets in Work Zone. To create a timesheet and enter leave:

1. Select the timesheet icon on the bottom of the screen.
2. Tap the timesheet area on the homepage.

3. Click on *Employees*.
4. Click on the *Manage Employees* tab.
5. Select *Create a Timesheet*.
6. Select the employee's name and select the week.
7. Select the *Work Time*. Put the start time, end time, break taken, and their location.
8. Click *Save*.
9. Click *Manage Employees*.
10. Select *Create Request* and choose the employee.
11. Select *Leave Category* and enter the period the employee will be on leave on the first and last days of the leave. The system will calculate and estimate the number of required leave days.
12. Click on *Approve Immediately*.

Creating Expenses for Employees

1. Click on Manage Employees.
2. Click on Create Expense Request.
3. Select the employee and the description of the expense being paid for
4. Input the expense date, the category, and the location. You can add a note choosing the tax code and the amount of the expense.
5. You can add an attachment that can be in the form of a pdf.
6. You can click on approve immediately or leave it empty and click on Create.
7. Now your expense request will reflect on the next payroll.

How Employees Can Self-Service

If an employer grants access to the portal, the employee will be instructed to activate their account and log in.

The following steps are for the employee to activate their account:

1. To begin, open the email inbox associated with the email address that you provided to your employer.
2. Find and open the email with the subject line "Login Information for Your Company Payroll."
3. To create a password, click on the link in the email you received.

4. Return to your email inbox and locate the email with the subject line "User Account Created."

5. In this email, you will be provided with the username for your portal account. This is the username for which you have created a password.

6. Click the email link that directs to the employee dashboard, which will take you to the login page.

7. To access the self-service portal, log into the portal using the password and the username

8. You now have access to the self-service portal. It's recommended that you bookmark the login page for easy access to the portal in the future.

How to Reset Your Password

If you have forgotten your password for the ESS Portal, follow the steps below to reset it.

1. Go to the Employee Self-Service Portal and log in.

2. Select *Forgotten Password* on the login page.

3. Enter your email address and select *Recover Password*.

4. A reset prompt will be sent to the email address provided during the signup.

5. Open the email and select the link to reset your password.

6. Create a new password and enter it a second time to confirm the password.

7. Select *Set Password*.

8. Select the link to log back into the portal.

9. Enter your email and new password to log in.

THE WORK ZONE APP FOR EMPLOYEES

Work Zone integrates with QuickBooks payroll, allowing employees to access self-service on their Android or iOS device.

Setting the Work Zone App for Employees

1. Download Work Zone from the Google Play Store on Android or the App Store on iOS.
2. Enter the email address and password to log in to access your employee service portal.
3. Create a pin that you will use each time you open the app.

Getting Around the Work Zone

To access the menu, click the hamburger icon. You can do a variety of things from here, including:

- Logging out of the app.
- Viewing login settings in the gear button.
- Viewing your own personal payroll details on employees list.
- View the business access.

Contents on the Home Screen

- Any content which requires employee acknowledgment
- Leave balances
- The last payslips
- Timesheet
- Expense summary
- Next shift time

Contents in the Profile Icon

- Employee details
- Bank account
- Payment summaries
- Super funds
- Leave
- Emergency contacts
- Other documents

If you log out of the app, you will be prompted to enter your email address, password, and PIN to re-enter it. If you exit the app and return later, you will only need to enter your PIN.

Enabling Work Zone

This feature is not enabled by default. You will enable it in the business portal so that employees can use it from their smartphones. You must navigate to *Payroll Settings* and then *Employee Portal Settings*.

☑ Employees can clock in/out using WorkZone

    ☑ Capture employee photo when clocking in/out

    ☑ Allow employees to select a higher classification when clocking in

The first step is to check the box next to "Employees can clock in/out using WorkZone."

The sub-settings in the picture below the first step are optional, but clearly affect the employee process when clocking in and out. After that send reminder emails to employees.

CHAPTER 9

INVENTORY

HOW TO SET UP INVENTORY TRACKING

QuickBooks has everything you need to manage your inventory. Track your inventory, receive reminders when it's time to refill, and gain insights into what you sell and buy. Non-inventory items and services can also be included so that they can be swiftly added to sales forms.

To enable inventory tracking, follow these steps:

1. Go to *Settings* and select *Accounts and Settings*.
2. Select *Sales*.
3. Select *Edit* in the Product and Service section.

4. Click *Show Product or Service* column on Sales Forms.
5. Click on both *Track Quantity and Price*, and *Track Inventory Quantity on Hand.*
6. Select *Save* and then *Done.*

Keep a record of what sells. When you've set up all of your inventory goods, you can track when they sell. There are two methods for keeping track of what you sell:

1. If you expect to be paid later, create an invoice.
2. If a customer pays on the spot, add a sales receipt.

The invoice or sales receipt reduces the amount on hand in QuickBooks.

To Check What's on Hand and Order as You Work

1. Click on the quantity of the item you entered to see more.
2. QuickBooks will notify you when items are running low or out of stock if you also set a low stock alert.

To Check Low Stock

QuickBooks detects when a product is running short if it is at or below its "reorder point," or the point at which you should reorder new stock.

When you add new items, you may input reorder points. If your existing goods lack reorder points, you may change them to include them.

You can order the things that are most important to you first. Here's how to verify if you have low stock or out of stock products once you've set up your reorder points.

1. Click Products and services from the Get paid & pay menu.
2. You can easily identify if you have low stock or out of stock at the top. To see those products, choose Low stock or Out of stock.

Restocking Your Inventory

When it's time to restock, you can use QuickBooks to order stock and keep track of what you've received from suppliers and what's on order. The quantity on hand will automatically increase due to the number of products you receive.

To create and send a purchase order, follow these steps:

1. Select *Sales.*
2. Click on *Products and Services.*
3. Select *Out of Stock.* Do not use any other filter to reorder low-stock and out-of-stock items from the same supplier.
4. Select the product at the top of the list. You will see a dropdown menu above the list of products.
5. Select the Batch action, then *Reorder.* It will create a purchase order for one supplier.
6. Complete all the required information on the purchase order.
7. Select *Save* and then *Send.*

Tracking What You've Received from the Vendor

Keep track of the products you've ordered. Go to Business Overview, then Reports, or go to Reports. After that, locate and run the Open Purchase Order Detail report.

You can check how many things are still on order and how many you've gotten so far in this section.

The two methods for tracking items received from the supplier are described below.

1. If you intend to pay later, create a bill from a purchase order.
2. If you paid your supplier on the spot, write a cheque or an expense from the purchase order.

This informs QuickBooks that you restocked, and the number of items received will increase the quantity in QuickBooks.

HOW TO CREATE CATEGORIES AND SUBCATEGORIES

Grouping items in QuickBooks help to organize products and services in the program.

Creating a Category

Categories are used to group items/products of the same type together. Subcategories can be created if you want to be more specific.

1. Go to the *Sales* menu.
2. Select *Products and Services*.
3. Select *More* and then *Manage Categories*.
4. Select *New Category*, then enter the category's name. If you need to create subcategories, select *Subcategory Box* and then the *Main Category*.
5. Click *Save*.

Categorize Products and Services

When you add a new inventory product, service, or non-inventory item, you can add it to a category by selecting it.

If you have uncategorized items, the instructions below will show you how to categorize them.

1. Go to the *Sales* menu, then select *Products or Services.*
2. Find the product or service to categorize.
3. Select *Edit* on the action column.
4. Select the category that fits the terms or add a new one to create a new one.
5. Click on *Save* and close

HOW TO ADD PRODUCTS MANUALLY

1. To add inventory items, turn on the inventory tracking.
2. Add your product's name and category. Once every setting is in place, you can add a product.
3. Go to *Sales*, then *Products and Services*.

4. Click on *New* or *Additional Products and Services.*

5. Select *Inventory.*

6. Add a name or category of what you are tracking.

7. Select the unit from the unit dropdown.

8. Select the category.

Adding a Product's Quantity, Reorder Point, and Inventory Asset Account

1. Go to the Sales>Product & Services>Inventory

2. Add the available product, followed by the date you started tracking that quantity.

3. You can add a reorder point to get alerts if it is time to reorder.

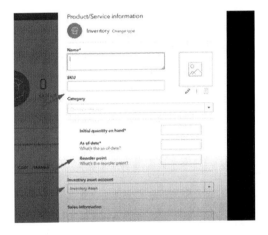

4. Select the *Inventory Asset Account* and click *Inventory Asset.* QuickBooks uses this account to track the inventory value.

Adding a Product's Sales, Tax, and Purchasing Details

In the same window of Inventory, at the bottom you will see details about product sales tax info and purchasing details. Here you can put all those details.

1. Add your product's description on the sales form. This will reflect on customers' invoices, sales receipts, and other forms.

2. Add the unit price followed by the sales price.

3. Select *Income Account* and find the account you use to track what you sell.
4. Choose the *Inclusive of the Tax* option if required or essential.
5. Select the *Tax Category* and how the item should be taxed. If you do not see this, set up the sales tax on QuickBooks.
6. Add your product's description on the purchase forms. It will show on bills, purchase orders, and other forms you send to suppliers.
7. Add the product's cost. If it changes, you can still enter the latest price when buying products.
8. Scroll down and select *Cost of Goods Sold* from the expense account.
9. Select the *Inclusive Purchase Tax* if required.
10. From the *Purchase Tax*, select the applicable purchase tax.
11. Add *Reverse Charge*.
12. Select a preferred supplier.
13. Select advance options.
14. Add a category for what you are tracking.
15. Select *Save* and then close.

IMPORT PRODUCTS AND SERVICES INTO QUICKBOOKS ONLINE

QuickBooks financial management software includes options for running spreadsheet data within the QuickBooks portal.

QuickBooks can import worksheets saved in Excel spreadsheet format directly into the program.

You may save time by importing a spreadsheet listing your services and products into QuickBooks. Following this guide, you'll be able to import a spreadsheet created in Excel or Google Sheets into QuickBooks with ease.

Format your Spreadsheet

In Excel or Google Sheets, you may construct a spreadsheet listing your products and services. The QuickBooks sample file demonstrates how to prepare your spreadsheet so that it imports properly. Here's how to get the QuickBooks Online sample file and formatting tips:

1. Login to QuickBooks Online.
2. Click Settings. Now choose Import Data.

3. Click Download a sample file and then open the file.

Tips for formatting:

-   Product/Service Name: has a character restriction of 100. Special characters should be avoided.
-   Income Account: Sub-accounts are not permitted.
-   Quantity as-of Date: In this format: DD/MM/YYYY or MM/DD/YYYY
-   Income and Expense account: subaccounts are not permitted.

Uploading a Spreadsheet to QuickBooks

Now that you've created a spreadsheet in Excel or Google Sheets containing your items and services, you're ready to import them into QuickBooks. Remember that once you import a list, it cannot be reversed. Furthermore, you can only import 1,000 rows at a time. If your list is larger than that, divide it into smaller files.

This is how you import your file:

1. Login to QuickBooks Online.
2. Choose Settings. Then choose Import Data.
3. Choose Products and Services.
4. To upload a file from your computer, select Browse. Select the file and then click Open.
5. To upload from Google Sheets, choose Connect and sign in using your Google account. Select the file after selecting it.
6. Select Next.
7. Organize your data. Your Field represents the spreadsheet's headers. Choose the option that corresponds to a field in QuickBooks Online from each drop-down menu.
8. Select Next.
9. If certain cells are marked in red, this indicates that the cell is invalid. Check your spreadsheet cell and try importing again.
10. For each product or service with the same name, choose Overwrite all values. Check that everything is in order because this cannot be undone.
11. Click Import.

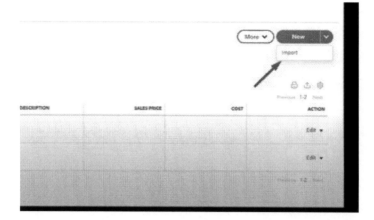

| CHAPTER 10 |

INSIGHTS AND REPORTS

| HOW TO CUSTOMIZE REPORTS

Reports contain a wealth of information about the business. Reports can be customized in a variety of ways, including:

- Filter them to show only certain accounts or customers.
- Format the layout so that the correct data appears in the correct place.

Types of Financial Reports in QuickBooks

- Balance Sheet
- Profit and Loss
- Cash Flow

Running A Report

1. Go to *Reports*.
2. Find and open a report.
3. Adjust report date by using the basic filters on the report.
4. Select *Customize* in the top right-hand corner of the page.
5. This will open the customization menu automatically.

Customize A Report

Multiple filters can be used to customize a report; many reports have a set of filters, and some are only available on specific reports.

What can be changed:

1. Rows or Column section: This is accomplished by specifying which rows and columns appear on the report.
2. Select the customers, suppliers, accounts, and products that appear on the report in the Filter section.
3. Change the reporting period, accounting method, and the number of formats in the general section.

Saving Custom Reports

1. Select Customization.
2. Give your report a name.
3. Select Save.

HOW TO CUSTOMIZE A REPORT FOR PROFIT AND LOSS ACCOUNT

1. Click on the report's menu.
2. Choose *Report Center*.
3. Select the Standard tab bar.
4. Under the dropdown list, select *Company and Financials*.
5. Choose one of the profit and loss reports and click *Run*.
6. Once the profit and loss reports are displayed on the screen.

7. Click the Customize Report bar on top of the screen.
8. Under the customize report window, you can make any changes you want. For example, report basics like the dates, apply filters, font size, font color, and many more.
9. Click *Okay*.

Managing Customized Reports

1. Go to *Reports* and select the *Custom Report* tab.
2. Find the group on the list.
3. Select *Edit* in the *Action* column for the report you want to delete.
4. Click *Delete*.

HOW TO VIEW PROFIT AND LOSS

Profit and Loss Account

A QuickBooks report summarizes your revenue and costs over a specific period, such as a month, quarter, or year (in the case of a corporation). It provides a high-level overview of the net profit or net loss for the time under consideration.

An accrual-basis (A) profit and loss statement is a more accurate predictor of profitability than cash flow because it includes income and costs that you own or owe regardless of whether money changed hands in the transaction. For example, even if you have not yet paid for the items used in the job, the materials in each task reduce your net income. This provides a much better match between revenue and costs than cash flow.

Sample Profit and Loss Report

Paul's Plumbing
PROFIT AND LOSS
January - December 2021

		TOTAL
▼ Income	A	
Sales		2,234.00
Services		4,025.00
Total Income		**$6,259.00**
▼ Cost of Goods Sold	B	
Cost of Goods Sold		750.00
Supplies COGS		1,000.00
Total Cost of Goods Sold		**$1,750.00**
GROSS PROFIT		**$4,509.00**
▼ Expenses	C	
6100 Advertising Expense		120.00
6115 Bank Service Charges		48.00
Vehicle Expense		2,750.00
Total Expenses		**$2,918.00**
NET OPERATING INCOME		**$1,591.00**
▼ Other Income	D	
Late Fee Income		150.00
Total Other Income		**$150.00**
NET OTHER INCOME		**$150.00**
NET INCOME		**$1,741.00**

Profitability

The first section summarizes the revenue generated by selling items and services over a specific period. In 2021, Paul's Plumbing had a total revenue of $6,259.

The Value of Goods Sold

The second section goes over the costs of purchasing or manufacturing everything on offer.

Operating Costs

The third section goes over the firm's non-COGS costs for the year. Paul's 2020 expenses came to $2,918. Net operating income is the difference between gross profit and operating expenses.

Other Sources of Revenue/Expenses

The final section includes revenue and costs unrelated to the business's normal operations. Customer late fees were classified as other revenue by Paul's Plumbing. Net income, also known as profit, is calculated by adding net operating income to any other revenue and subtracting costs.

HOW TO CREATE A PROFIT AND LOSS STATEMENT IN QUICKBOOKS

In QuickBooks, the income statement may be generated in four simple stages.

1. In the left menu, click Reports.
2. In the *Business Overview* section, click *Profit and Loss*.
3. By scrolling up, you can view and modify the profit and loss report settings.
4. Select Customize to further personalize the report.
5. Click an email, print, or export the Profit and Loss Report in the report's top right corner.

HOW TO PLAN YOUR CASHFLOW

This report summarizes the net amount of cash and cash equivalents moved into and out of business.

Cash Flow Planner

The Cash Flow Planner is a valuable tool for forecasting your company's cash flow, cash outflows, and cash inflows. It examines your financial history to forecast future cash-in and cash-out transactions. Furthermore, you can add or edit future events to see how different changes affect your cash flow.

Changes to events in the planner have no impact or update on your books. This enables the owner to make sound financial decisions regarding saving, spending, borrowing, and transferring funds. Among these considerations are:

- What exactly is forecasting, and how does it function?
- What information does this report contain?

The cash flow planner chart forecasts expected income and spending by analyzing previous data from your QuickBooks Online-linked bank accounts. This category includes transactions that are both classified and unclassified. Furthermore, you can manually incorporate data to forecast cash flow by adding future events.

The cash flow planner graphic does not include the following elements:

- Credit card transactions
- Trust fund transactions
- Manually entered transactions into QuickBooks
- Files with multi-currency support

Note: When you disconnect a bank account, the data on the chart disappears.

- Choose Money in if the event is an income event and Money out if it is an expense event.
- Enter a name for the event and an amount, then click Continue.
- Choose the date and time of the event.
- When you're finished, click Save.

To change or remove an event:

1. Choose and then open an event.
2. Change the Date, Merchant Name, or Amount box, or toggle between Money in and Money out.
3. When you're finished, click Save.

How to Create a Cash Flow Statement

1. Click the "Reports" menu
2. Choose "Statement of Cash Flows".
3. Choose "Standard".

How to Use the Cash Flow Planner

A cash flow planner is a tool that forecasts future cash flow in and out of your business based on historical data.

Here are the steps on how to use the cash flow planner:

1. In the *Navigator* tab, select the *Cash Flow* menu

2. Choose *Planner*.
3. To configure your planner, implement the on-screen instructions.
4. Once the planner is set up, select the date filters to set the forecast range.
5. Select the *Cash Flow In and Out* and *Cash Balance Filter* to filter the list.
6. Click the bar and drag it across the chart to a specific date.

How to Edit and Delete Items in Cash Flow Planner

1. In the "*Navigator* tab, select the *Cash Flow* menu.
2. Choose the *Planner* tab
3. Select items for editing or deletion.
4. If you are editing an item, make the necessary changes you want to make, then click *Okay* to save.
5. Select "Delete" if you need to delete the item.

How to View Cash Inflows and Outflows

1. In the *Navigator* tab, select the *Cash Flow* menu.
2. Click the *Overview* tab.
3. Choose view to see open invoices and bills that generate cash, or view reports to see a summary of all unpaid invoices and bills.

| CHAPTER 11 |

MOBILE APP

| HOW TO SEND A QUOTE USING THE APP

QuickBooks Online is compatible with iOS and Android, allowing you to access your business information no matter where you are.

First, download the QuickBooks mobile app from iTunes or Google Play, depending on whether you have an iPhone or Android.

1. Log in to your QuickBooks using your username and password.
2. Use your QuickBooks details to sign into the app. The display on your device will be like that on the browser.
3. To create quotes, click on the plus sign, then select *Quotes*.

4. Select the customer and input the relevant information for the quote.
5. Email the quotation to the client.
6. The customer accepts the quote by signing on the iPhone or Android phone screen. This is done by clicking on *Get Signature*.
7. The customers will use their fingers or stylus to sign on the screen.
8. Click *Done* to save the quote updated. The signature captured will be saved as an attachment to the customer quote.

HOW TO SEND AN INVOICE USING THE APP

1. Open your mobile up and go to the Shortcut menu.
2. Select *Invoices* and then select *Add New Invoice* near the bottom of the screen
3. In the first field, select the customer or project you are invoicing. If it is a new customer, select *Add* near the bottom of the screen.
4. If you choose an existing customer, you can either assign a new invoice number or leave it blank, and the QuickBooks mobile app will assign a new invoice number in the sequence.
5. Depending on how you configure QuickBooks, today's date will be displayed automatically.
6. Next, select *Add Product or Service*. The app will display the list of products and services you are dealing with.
7. Enter the quality and rate you want to appear on your invoices.
8. Enter the applicable tax code for the product.
9. Select *Add* upon completion of product or service update, after which an invoice will display.
10. Select *Save* after inputting all the required details, and you will notice a confirmation that an invoice has been created.

Sending an Invoice Using a Mobile App

1. Select Send Invoice.
2. QuickBooks will retrieve the customer's email address and display the subject line and email message to customize if desired. You can see the invoice preview that customers will see if they open the email by scrolling down.
3. When you press the send button, you will see the invoice status and the date it was sent. The status will be updated when the customer views the

Invoice. You will also receive payment and deposit updates if you have a payment setup, and your bank is linked to a QuickBooks account.

HOW TO USE RECEIPT CAPTURE

1. Sign in QuickBooks on your android phone or iPhone using your online user ID and password once you are signed in.
2. Go to *Menu*.
3. Tap *Receipt Capture*, and it will automatically open the camera. Take a photo of your receipt or bill.

4. Select *Use this photo* once you are satisfied with the receipt captured. You will receive a notification that the receiver has been uploaded on your phone.

5. Go to your QuickBooks Online.

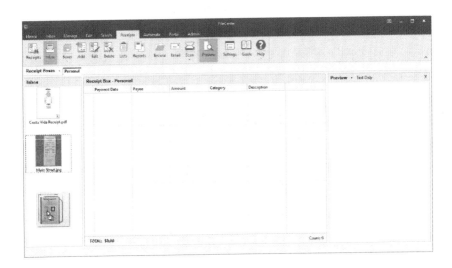

6. Select *Banking* and click on *Receipts*.

Here is what you should do if QuickBooks discovers one or more transactions that match your submitted receipt or bill:

1. Click a receipt that will provide a list of the transactions that correspond with it.

2. Select the transaction you wish to associate with the receipt or the bill.

When a receipt or bill does not have a label next to the amount, it simply means QuickBooks could not locate an existing transaction that matches it. You can only create a new transaction using your receipt or bill as the basis.

1. Select the receipt or bill.

2. Create an expense or bill.

If the Receipt or Bill Has Missing Information

This indicates that QuickBooks has not extracted all necessary information from a receipt or bill and requires additional data or specifications before issuing a bill.

1. Select Expenses from the left menu in QuickBooks Online.
2. Select Expense from the Type drop-down after clicking the Filter drop-down.
3. Choose the date range for the transactions you wish to display, then click Apply.
4. Open each transaction in the list to see which ones have a missing receipt attachment.
5. Then, if any attachments are missing, add them.

Made in the USA
Monee, IL
16 June 2024

59942627R00116